THE ARMCHAIR REFEREE

THE ARMCHAIR REFEREE—
500 Questions and answers
about football

JERRY MARKBREIT

DOUBLEDAY & COMPANY, INC.
Garden City, New York
1973

ACKNOWLEDGMENTS

It won't be possible to list all of the people who have helped me in the writing of this book, but I thank them from the bottom of my heart. I would particularly like to thank Herm Rohrig, supervisor of officials for the Big Ten Conference; Violet Frankel, secretary extraordinaire; Jim Mullen, sports editor for the Chicago *Sun-Times;* Herman Kogan, editor of the Chicago *Sun-Times Showcase* magazine; and my good friend Frank Strocchia, commissioner of the Chicago Catholic League.

796.33
M

ISBN: 0-385-08089-1
Library of Congress Catalog Card Number 73–81414
Copyright © 1973 by Jerry Markbreit
All Rights Reserved
Printed in the United States of America
First Edition

TO MY WONDERFUL FAMILY.
THEIR PATIENCE AND UNDERSTANDING MADE IT ALL
POSSIBLE.

BOBBIE   KATHY   BETSY

INTRODUCTION

by

WAYNE DUKE, *Commissioner of the Big Ten Athletic Conference*

My past experience and my present position have always required providing answers to a variety of sports questions. Although the questions involved are often confusing or perplexing, an immediate answer is possible because of experience or the immediate availability of a rule book. Questions demand answers. The answers are normally acceptable only from someone who is recognized as an authority. That is exactly what you have in the author of this book. He is technically qualified to provide the answers to the most controversial portion of football: the rules of the game.

Football has often been mistaken for an uncomplicated game. The very opposite is true. The rules of the game, unless you are a member of the Rules Committee or an official with years of experience, are most difficult to master. As is so often said, the shape of the ball causes a variety of strange bounces, each of which creates a new rule situation. The rule book alone demands many years of concentrated study and must be constantly reviewed from year to year because of the rules changes involved. It all boils down to the fact that a true understanding of football requires years of active experience. Or, alternately, one can have a book that, because of the author's experience and study, provides the answers to any situation that may arise on the field. This book is now a reality. It provides the answers to over five hundred pro and college football questions. The book is written in language that can be understood by those who consider themselves authorities on the rules as well as by individuals who have no previous knowledge of the game.

Do you have a football question? The answer is at your fingertips. Just turn the pages and there it is.

WAYNE DUKE
Commissioner Big Ten Athletic Conference

CONTENTS

PREFACE

It usually takes a minute or two at the most to open your back door, carry out your garbage, put it into the trash can, and return to the friendly confines of your humble abode. But wait just a minute! What does that have to do with football? It has no direct connection with the gridiron, but it is one of the reasons why I have written this book.

When I throw out my garbage it usually takes thirty to forty minutes, and my trash cans are only two feet from my back door. No, I don't have that much garbage, but I do have a very avid and astute football fan for a next-door neighbor. He is always waiting for me with a list of questions a foot and a half long. He's there in the rain and in subzero weather. He wants answers about football, and I have been giving them to him for several years. The more knowledgeable he becomes, the more questions he asks. He's quite a guy.

I decided to write this book for him and all the other football fans around the country with lists of questions and no one around to answer them.

Football is just plain complicated. The rules of the game are a life's work to master and, as luck would have it, the college game has one set of rules while the professional game has another. Do you know what the referee is saying with his arm signals? Do you know the difference between the pro and college rules? Do you know that a great play on Saturday afternoon may be a foul on Sunday afternoon or Monday night? I wonder how many of you can answer these questions? Whether you can or cannot really makes no difference. That's what makes football so wonderful. All you have to do is watch the ball and the officials will do the rest.

In the following pages you will find just about everything you ever wanted to know about football, both professional and college. There should be something of interest for everyone.

This book will help the knowledgeable fan as well as the beginner. It has been written for you, and I hope you enjoy it as much as I have enjoyed writing it.

April 1973   JERRY MARKBREIT

THE ARMCHAIR REFEREE

DEFINITIONS

We all know how important it is to have an in-depth vocabulary in our everyday life. It is equally important to have a complete knowledge of football definitions if we are to become truly knowledgeable football fans.

Unless you have a neighbor who is an official or a friend who is completely versed in the rules of the game, this book will become your best friend. It will make you the neighborhood authority on football rules. A word of warning! Don't expect to be able to walk onto any college or pro football field and think you are qualified to officiate a football game. Please do yourself a favor and confine your newly acquired knowledge to your living room or den. It takes many years of experience to correctly administer these rules in the heat of battle.

These definitions will provide you with the knowledge necessary to intelligently discuss the rules of the game and make you the football "expert" of your block.

ACTION PASS: Forward pass thrown from a simulated running formation.

AUDIBLE (Automatic): Changing the play called in the huddle with a vocal signal at the line of scrimmage.

BACK: A player who is legally behind the scrimmage line when the ball is snapped. All backs except the quarterback must be at least one yard behind the line at the snap. The quarterback, if he is in a position to receive a hand-to-hand snap from the center, may be less than one yard behind the line.

BACKWARD PASS: Any pass that does not go forward, *including a lateral pass*.

BALANCED LINE: When three linemen are on either side of the center.

BALL BOYS: The men or boys who walk the sidelines carrying an extra ball, which they give to the nearest official when the game ball goes out of bounds or is overthrown.

BALL CARRIER: Runner.

"BALL GOES OVER": Offensive team fails to make a first down and the defense takes over.

BATTING: Striking the ball with the hands or arms.

BETWEEN DOWNS: The interval during which the ball is dead between plays.

BLIND-SIDE BLOCK: A block made from an angle that makes it impossible for the player being blocked to see the blocker.

BLITZ (Red Dog): Any number of defensive backs or linebackers committed to rushing the passer.

BLOCKING: The legal means of obstructing an opponent by contacting him with any part of the blocker's body.

BOMB: A very long forward pass.

BOOTLEG: When the quarterback runs in the opposite direction from the offensive flow and hides the ball along his thigh.

BOUNDARY LINES: The end lines and the sidelines. These lines run around the outside edge of the field. The boundary lines are all out of bounds.

BOX MAN: The individual responsible for the down indicator. Before each play he takes a position at the forward point of the ball with the correct number of the down showing on the indicator.

NOTE: The name "box man" comes from the fact that the first-down indicator was box-shaped, with the numbers 1 through 4 showing on the individual sides.

BREAD-AND-BUTTER PLAY: A play that "always" gains a few yards.

BULLET PASS: A pass that is thrown very hard and remains parallel with the ground.

BUTTONHOOK PATTERN: Pass receiver goes downfield and then turns in the direction of the line to catch the pass.

CATCH: The act of gaining possession of a live ball in flight. Under college rules the player who jumps into the air to make a catch must have the ball in his possession when he first returns to the ground inbounds. One foot is sufficient for a completed pass. Under pro rules the player catching the ball must have touched the ground inbounds with both feet before it can be ruled a completed pass.

CHAIN CREW: This is made up of the two chain men and the box man, and is under the direction of the head linesman.

CHAIN MEN: The two individuals responsible for the proper movement of the chain. They each have a stake separated by a chain ten yards long. This chain is the distance required by rule for a team to gain a first down.

CLIPPING: Throwing the body across the back of the legs of an opponent or charging or falling into the back of an opponent after approaching him from the rear unless he is the ball carrier or unless he is in the legal clip zone.

COACH: A coach is a man charged with enormous responsibility. He must be of very strong character. He must possess the qualities of an executive, a public relations man, a salesman, a professor, a chaplain, a psychiatrist, a philosopher, and last but most important, a strategist. His position demands patience with varying degrees of firmness. He must have the hide of an elephant to cope with the pressures to "win at all costs." He must be able to deal with the news media, the fans, and the alumni if he is a college coach. The coach dedicates his life to his profession, and in doing so deprives himself and his family of the normal family life. He puts in a ten-to-fifteen-hour day, seven days a week in his attempt to succeed in his profession. The pressures on the coach of today have forced him to change his philosophy toward the game. "It's not how we played the game, it's whether we won or lost." Unfortunately, these pressures common to the sports scene have caused most coaching positions in pro and college ball to be in constant jeopardy. The coach must field a winner to remain in his capacity. Win or else!

COFFIN CORNER: The area near the intersection of the sideline and goal line in the field of play.

COMPLETE PASS (Complete): A pass that is caught inbounds by a member of the offensive team.

CONTINUING ACTION: Any player action occurring immediately after the ball has been declared dead.

CRAWLING: COLLEGIATE RULES: An attempt by the runner to advance the ball after any part of his body, except hands or feet, has touched the ground.

PRO RULES: An attempt by a runner to advance after any part of his body, except hands or feet, has touched the ground, providing he has been contacted by a defensive player.

CUTBACK: When a player heads for the outside and suddenly changes his direction to the inside.

DEAD BALL: A ball not in play.

DEFENSIVE TEAM: The opposing team. The team not in possession of the ball.

DISQUALIFIED PLAYER: A player who is banned from further play in the game.

DIVE PLAY: A short gain up the middle.

DOUBLE TEAMING: Two offensive linemen blocking one defensive man or two defensive men guarding one offensive receiver.

DOWN (Play): A unit of the game that starts when the ball is put in play and ends when the ball is declared dead.

DOWN AND OUT: Offensive receiver runs straight downfield and cuts to the outside.

DRAW: Quarterback starts to drop back to pass but hands off to a running back who delayed in the backfield.

DROP KICK: A kick by a player who drops the ball and kicks it as it touches the ground or as it is rising from the ground.

EAT THE BALL: Quarterback is tackled before he can pass the ball.

END LINES: The white lines running the width of the field at the back of the end zones.

END ZONE: That area bounded by the goal line, end line, and sidelines.

FAIR CATCH: An unhindered catch by any member of the receiving team, of any kick that has crossed the kicker's scrimmage or free kick line, provided that a proper signal has been given.

FAIR CATCH SIGNAL: PRO RULE: One hand raised and at full arm's length above the head.

COLLEGIATE RULE: Extending one hand and one arm above the head and waving them from side to side.

FIELD GOAL: Made by kicking the ball from the field of play by drop kick or place kick so that the ball goes over the crossbar and between the uprights of the defending team's goal post.

FIELD MARKER OR PYLON: Flag or flexible rubber standard used to mark the intersections of the sidelines and the goal lines.

FIRST DOWN AND TEN: A series of four consecutive downs are given to the team that will next put the ball in play by a snap from center following a free kick, touchback, fair catch, or change of team possession. They must gain ten yards in four downs in order to keep possession of the ball.

"FLAG": The penalty marker used by a game official. Pro officials use a yellow flag. College officials use a combination red and white flag. Often referred to as the "rag" by most officials.

FLAG PATTERN: Pass receiver runs directly toward the field marker flag at the intersection of the goal line and the sideline.

FLANKER: Backfield man who is stationed wide to either side of the field as a pass receiver.

FLARE: Pass pattern to a receiver who swings wide from a backfield position.

FLOOD AN AREA: When many eligible pass receivers run to the same general area on a pass play.

FORWARD PASS: Under PRO RULES it is a pass that goes toward the opposing team's goal line. Under COLLEGIATE RULES it is a pass that strikes anything beyond the spot of the pass.

FORWARD PROGRESS (Progress Point): The most forward point that the ball is advanced toward the opponents' goal line when the ball is declared dead.

FOUL: An infraction of the rules for which a penalty is prescribed.

FREE BALL: A ball in play but not in possession or control of any player.

FREE KICK: A kick made under certain restrictions. The kicking team may not advance beyond their free kick line and the receiving team may not advance beyond their restraining line until the ball is kicked.

FREE KICK DOWN: A down that starts with a free kick.

FREE KICK LINE FOR KICKERS: A yard line through the most forward point from which the ball may be kicked.

FREE KICK LINE FOR RECEIVERS: A yard line ten yards in advance of kicker's free kick line.

FRONT FOUR: A four-man defensive front line.

FUMBLE: Loss of possession by a player of either team other than by passing it or kicking the ball. In order to fumble the ball, it must be in possession.

GOAL LINE: A vertical plane separating the end zone from the field of play. A team's goal line is the one they are defending.

GOAL TO GO: When a new series begins with less than ten yards to gain because the spot of the snap is less than ten yards from the opponents' goal line.

HANDOFF: The act of handing the ball directly to another player, usually from a back to a back.

HANDLING THE BALL: Changing player possession from one to another without fumbling, kicking, or throwing the ball.

HUDDLE: Two or more offensive players grouped together behind the line of scrimmage for the purpose of getting the next play from the *quarterback*. Two or more defensive players grouped together behind their line of scrimmage in order to get the defensive formation to be used.

ILLEGAL HURDLING: An attempt by a runner to jump over an opponent who is on his feet.

IMPETUS: Force provided by a player or a team that is responsible for the action of the ball.

INBOUND LINES (Hashmarks): The white lines parallel to the sidelines. PRO RULES have them 70'9" from the sidelines. COLLEGIATE RULES have them 53'4" from the sidelines.

INBOUNDS: The area within the playing field.

INCOMPLETE PASS (Incomplete): A pass that is not caught by a member of either team; a pass that hits the ground or goes out of bounds not in player possession.

IN PLAY: When the ball is legally kicked or snapped.

KEYING: When a defender guides himself by the movements of a specific offensive lineman.

KICKER: Any player who punts, drop kicks, or place kicks the ball according to the rules of the game. He remains the kicker until he has had a reasonable amount of time to regain his balance.

KICKERS: Denotes all members of the kicking team.

KICKOFF: A free kick that starts each half and follows each extra point or successful field goal.

LATERAL PASS: Any pass that is thrown parallel to the line of scrimmage or any yard line.

LEGAL CLIP ZONE: COLLEGIATE RULES: A rectangular area centered on the middle lineman of the offensive team and extending four yards laterally in each direction and three yards on either side of the scrimmage line.

PRO RULES: Their clip zone covers close line play that occurs in an area extending laterally to the positions usually occupied by offensive tackles and three yards on either side of the line of scrimmage.

LINEBACKER: A defensive man positioned behind the line with the option of defending the run or covering pass receivers.

LINEMAN: A player who is on his scrimmage line when the ball is snapped.

LINE OF SCRIMMAGE: A yard line passing through the end of the ball nearest a team's own goal line. Each team has its own line of scrimmage. The distance between the offensive and defensive scrimmage line is the length of the football (11" to 11¼").

LINE POSITIONS: Ends, guards, tackles, and center.

LIVE BALL: A ball that is in play.

LONG MAN: The deepest offensive receiver on a pass play.

LOOK-IN PASS: Pass receiver goes diagonally downfield and immediately looks back for the ball.

LOSS OF DOWN: When the down just played counts, even if a penalty is accepted.

MAN-FOR-MAN COVERAGE: Pass defenders each take an offensive man and go wherever he goes during the play.

MONSTER MAN: A roving linebacker.

MUFF: An unsuccessful attempt to gain possession of a ball that is touched in the attempt.

NAILED: To be tackled very hard.

NEUTRAL ZONE: The space between the two scrimmage lines.

OFFENSIVE TEAM: The team in possession of the ball.

OFFICIAL: Why would a man of outstanding character want to subject himself to all the abuses heaped upon his shoulders by becoming a football official? Who is this strange creature who enjoys blowing a whistle and imposing penalties for infractions of the rules? He may be a rich man, a poor man, a doctor, a lawyer, a schoolteacher, an Indian chief or a butcher, a barber or even a candlestick maker. More often than not, however, this man is your next-door neighbor, your acquaintance at the grocery store, or the man who sits next to you in church. He may be the local Boy Scout troop leader or the guy who is always active in community affairs. In other words, he is just an average John Q. Citizen coming from all walks of life. He enjoys playing with his kids, taking his wife out on weekends, and all the other pleasures that make for a happy life. The only thing that makes an official a little different than most is his great love of sports and his ability to react with great precision under extreme pressure. He knows that he is not a necessary evil but a very vital and important part of the game. Without him we could have no contest. We owe him our respect.

OFFICIALS' WIVES: Very patient and understanding.

OFFSET (Offsetting Fouls): Each team fouls during a down. The down is replayed.

OFFSIDE: A player is offside when any part of his body is beyond the scrimmage line or free kick line when the ball is put into play. *Exceptions:* The center may be beyond his line as long as he is not beyond the defensive line. On a kickoff the holder and kicker may be beyond the free kick line.

ONSIDE KICK: An effort by the kicking team to kick short and recover their own kick after it has traveled ten yards.

ON THE LINE (Line): When offensive linemen are in position on their line of scrimmage. The defensive linemen may be anywhere behind their line of scrimmage at the snap.

OUT OF BOUNDS: When a player or the ball is not in the field of play or the end zone.

PASS: Throwing the ball.

PASS DEFENDER: A member of the defensive team whose job is to keep the receiver from catching a pass. He also tries to intercept the pass.

PASSER: A player who throws a legal forward pass.

PASS INTERCEPTION: When a pass is caught by a member of the opposing team.

PASS RECEIVER: A member of the offensive team who is designated to catch a forward or backward pass thrown by a teammate.

PAYDIRT: The end zone and the touchdown.

PENALTY: A loss imposed by rule against the team that has fouled.

PICK PLAY: An illegal screen. During a down in which a forward pass is thrown, an offensive receiver who is downfield attempts to screen a defensive backfield man but makes illegal contact. This contact is illegal because the offensive man is not permitted to contact the defense on a forward pass play from the time the ball is snapped until the ball is touched by either team.

PITCHOUT: Quarterback takes the ball, turns, and quickly throws a short underhand pass to one of his backs, who is usually in motion.

PLACE KICK: A kick by a player of the team in possession who kicks the ball from a fixed spot either on the ground or on a tee. The ball may be held in position by a man from the kicking team.

PLAYER: Any one of the twenty-two participants actually in the game at a particular time.

PLAYER IN POSSESSION: Holding or controlling a live ball.

POCKET: A protected area for a passer formed by his blockers behind his line of scrimmage.

POST PATTERN: Pass receiver runs directly toward opponents' goal post.

POWER PLAY: An offensive running play using mass blocking.

PREVENT DEFENSE: Defense uses less men up front and more deep defenders. The purpose is to give the offense the short gain but to reduce chances for a long gain.

PREVIOUS SPOT: The place where the last play began.

PRO: An abbreviation for a professional football player.

PULLING LINEMEN: Offensive linemen who pull out of the line for the purpose of trap blocking or leading a run.

PUNT: A kick by a player who drops the ball and kicks it before it strikes the ground.

QUARTERBACK: The offensive player who has the responsibility of directing his team's attack.

QUARTERBACK SNEAK: The quarterback takes the ball and runs up the middle.

QUICK OPENER: A short plunge into the line with no fake handoff by the quarterback.

RECEIVERS: Denotes all members of the receiving team.

RECOVERY (Recover): Gaining possession of a live ball after it has hit the ground.

RETURN KICK: A kick made by a player after his team has gained possession of the ball during a down. In other words, a kick by a team after they have recovered a fumble, intercepted a pass, or received a kick. Under COLLEGIATE RULES a return kick is an illegal kick. Under PRO RULES any number of return kicks may be made during a down.

REVERSE: A handoff from one player to another while they are moving in opposite directions.

ROLLOUT (Option Play): Quarterback runs laterally behind the line of scrimmage with an option to run or pass.

RUNNER: A player in possession of a live ball.

SAFETY: A situation in which the ball is dead on or behind a team's own goal line, provided the force that put the ball in the end zone came from the team defending that goal line.

SAFETYMAN: A deep defensive backfield man.

SCREEN PASS: A pass to a receiver who, after a slight delay, takes a position *behind the line* of scrimmage and behind a wall of blockers who have permitted defenders to penetrate un-molested toward the passer. The linemen are restricted by rule from advancing beyond the line until the pass is thrown.

SCRIMMAGE DOWN: A down that starts with a snap from the center.

SCRIMMAGE KICK: A kick by the offensive team during a scrimmage down before team possession changes.

SECONDARY: The defensive backfield.

SHIFT: The action of two or more offensive players before the snap, who, after having assumed a set position, simultaneously change their position. The defense can move any time as long as they are behind their line of scrimmage at the snap.

SHOESTRING TACKLE: A tackle around the ankles.

SIDELINES: The white lines running down either side of the field.

SIDE ZONES: The areas bounded by the goal lines, sidelines, and the lines parallel to the sidelines called inbound lines.

SLOTBACK: An offensive back positioned in the backfield between the wide receiver and an interior lineman.

SNAP: Handing or passing the ball back from its position on the ground with a quick continuous motion of the hand or hands.

SNAPPER OR CENTER: The player who snaps the ball.

SPEARING: Illegally using the head and helmet to blast into an opponent after his momentum has stopped.

SPOT OF ENFORCEMENT: The spot at which a penalty for a foul is enforced. The enforcement spot is not always the point of the infraction.

STIFF-ARM: A runner using an outstretched arm and hand to ward off a would-be tackler.

STRONG SIDE: When the offense positions more men on one side of the center than the other, causing an unbalanced line.

STUNTING: Defensive players changing positions as the ball is snapped.

SUBSTITUTE: A replacement for a player or one filling a player vacancy.

TACKLING: Grabbing or pulling an opponent to the ground with the hands or arms.

TAXI SQUAD: The term used to identify those pro players who are under contract to a team, who practice with that team, but who are not listed on the team's official roster. They can be activated if needed.

TEAM IN POSSESSION: A term used to indicate the holding or controlling of a live ball or a ball to be free kicked. Player possession dictates team possession when that player is attempting a punt, drop kick, or place kick or while a forward pass thrown by a team member is in flight.

TIGHT END: Offensive end who lines up very close to other interior linemen. Used as a blocker as well as a pass receiver.

TOUCHBACK: A situation in which the ball is dead on or behind a team's own goal line, provided the force that put the ball in the end zone came from an opponent of the team defending that goal line.

TOUCHDOWN: A situation in which any part of the ball, legally in possession of an in-bounds player, is above, on, or beyond the opponents' goal line.

TRAP BLOCKING: Permitting a defensive player to penetrate the line and then blocking him from the side.

TRAPPED PASS: A ball that is caught after it has touched the ground. If this happens on a pass play it is an incomplete pass.

TRIPPING: Use of the leg or foot to obstruct any opponent below the knees, including the runner.

TRY FOR POINT (Try, "Extra Point"): An opportunity given to a team that has just scored a touchdown to score one or two additional points during one scrimmage down. PRO RULES: The ball is snapped from the two-yard line. A run that would ordinarily score a touchdown scores one (1) point. A kick that would ordinarily score a field goal scores one (1) point. COL-LEGIATE RULES: The ball is snapped from the three-yard line. A run or completed pass for score will award two (2) points and a successful kick will score one (1) point.

TURNOVER: Loss of possession during a play.

VIOLATION: A rule infraction that carries no distinct penalty and that does not offset the penalty for a foul.

WALK-OFF: Slang expression for assessing a penalty.

WHISTLE: That thing the officials blow when a play is over.

WIDE RECEIVER: Flanker back or split end who is set out wide and is a potential pass receiver.

YARD LINE: Any line in the field of play parallel to the end line.

ZONE COVERAGE: Defensive men cover specific areas instead of specific men.

SIGNALS

The dictionary defines the word "signal" as a means of communicating instructions, commands, warnings, directions, etc., by using signs, arm signals, flags, lights, etc. Football officials use arm signals for most of these reasons. With the tremendous amount of noise generated by the huge crowds of today, it would be impossible to communicate in any other way in the time allowed.

We officials have our own special sign language and, unfortunately, most football fans haven't done their homework where signals are concerned. It won't take long to learn the meanings of the signals, and once you do, you'll wonder why you waited so long.

The professional football signals and the college football signals are basically similar, but there are some differences. Both sets of signals are illustrated and defined in this chapter.

When the referee steps out into the open next season and places both hands on the top of his head, you will know instantly that he is signaling ineligible receiver downfield if it is a pro game and illegal substitution if it's a college game. When he touches his hands to his shoulders you will know that he has an illegal touching violation in college football and a loss-of-down penalty in pro football.

You will be watching the game like a true expert. You won't have to wait for an explanation from the sportscaster or field announcer to know what is going on because you will be reading the signals as well as anyone.

PRO OFFICIALS' SIGNALS

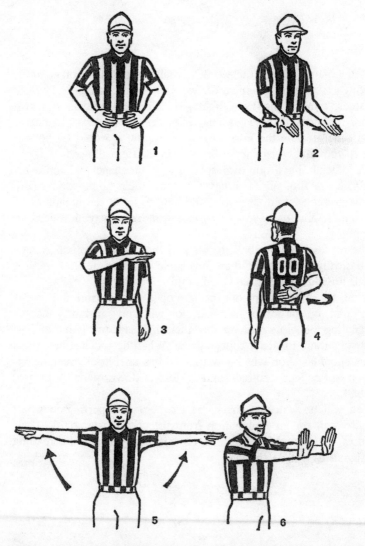

1. Offside **2.** Crawling, Helping the runner **3.** Illegal motion of offensive player at snap **4.** Illegal forward pass, Intentional grounding (also passing motion) **5.** Unsportsmanlike conduct **6.** Forward pass interference, Kick catch interference

7. Holding or illegal use of hands or arms **8.** Personal foul (all acts that are unnecessarily rough) **9.** Running into or roughing the kicker (must be preceded by personal foul signal) **10.** Running into passer (must be preceded by personal foul signal) **11.** Tripping (must be preceded by personal foul signal) **12.** Clipping (must be preceded by personal foul signal)

13. Delay of game (taking too long to put the ball into play) **14.** Illegal formation **15.** Touchdown, Field goal is good, Try is good **16.** Safety **17.** Loss of the down **18.** Incomplete pass, Penalty declined, No score

19. First down **20.** Ball is dead, Neutral zone established **21.** No time out, Time is in when whistle blows

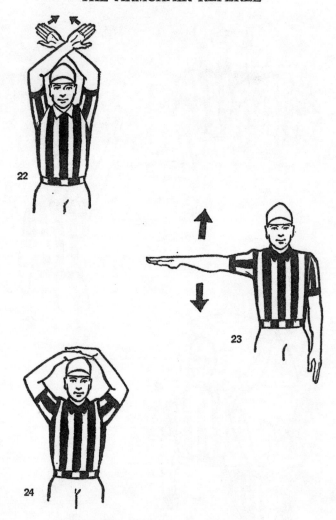

22. Time out, Official's time out by also putting one hand on cap **23.** Touchback (must be preceded by time-out signal) **24.** Ineligible receiver downfield on forward pass

COLLEGIATE OFFICIALS' SIGNALS

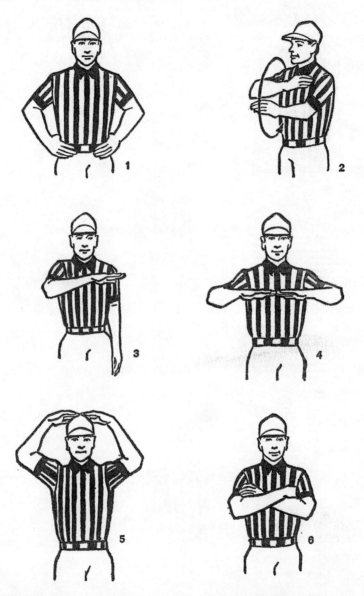

1. Offside 2. Illegal position, Illegal procedure 3. Illegal motion of an offensive player at the snap 4. Illegal shift (illegal movement of two or more offensive men) 5. Substitution foul 6. Delay of game (taking too long to put the ball into play)

7. Personal foul (all acts that are unnecessarily rough) **8.** Clipping
9. Roughing the kicker **10.** Unsportsmanlike conduct (noncontact)

11. Holding (illegally using the hands or arms) **12.** Intentional grounding of a forward pass **13.** Illegal forward pass, Illegally handing ball forward **14.** Forward pass interference, Kick catch interference **15.** Ineligible pass receiver downfield on forward pass **16.** Illegally touching, Batting, or Kicking the ball

17. Incomplete pass, Penalty declined, No score **18.** Helping the runner, Blockers locking arms or legs **19.** Ball is dead. If hand and arm are moved from side to side it is a touchback **20.** Touchdown, Field goal is good, Try is good **21.** Safety

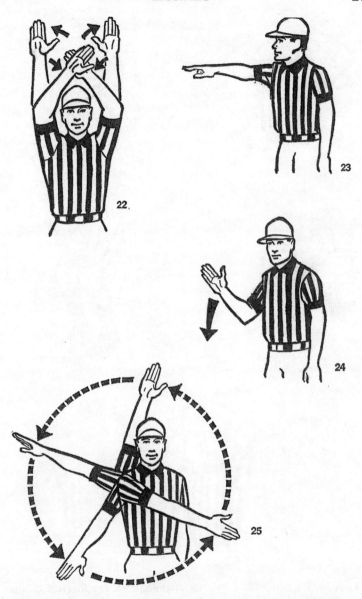

22. Time out, Official's time out by also touching hands to chest **23.** First down **24.** Ball is ready for play **25.** Start the clock

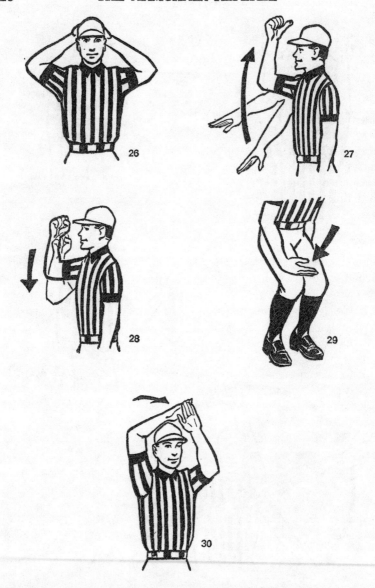

26. Loss of the down **27.** Player disqualified (out for the rest of the game) **28.** Grabbing the face mask **29.** Crack back block below waist (not a clip) **30.** Player touching a forward pass or a kick

THE FIELD

American football fields are 360 feet long and 160 feet wide. Now, we all know that football fields are 100 yards long, and 100 yards is less than 360 feet. The answer to this is end zone yardage. Each end zone is 30 feet or 10 yards.

American football fields have end zones, end lines, sidelines, yard lines, inbound lines, flags or pylons, goal posts, and limit lines. To the average fan a field is a field, whether he is watching a college game on Saturday or a pro game on Sunday or Monday.

Actually, there are major differences between college and pro fields. The diagrams will illustrate the differences, but I will list them here so you won't have to search too hard.

1. College goal posts are on the end line. Pro goal posts are on the goal line.

2. College goal posts are 23'4" wide. Pro goal posts are 18'6" wide.

3. College inbound lines (hashmarks) are 53'4" from the sidelines. Pro inbounds lines are 70'9" from the sidelines.

4. Try for point or "extra point" in college ball is snapped from the 3-yard line. The pros snap it from the 2-yard line.

5. The pros' field has a dot or some special mark 10'9" wider than their inbounds line only on each 15-, 10-, and 5-yard line for punting situations. The college field has no such markings.

After careful study of the following diagrams, you will immediately spot the differences when attending or viewing your next game.

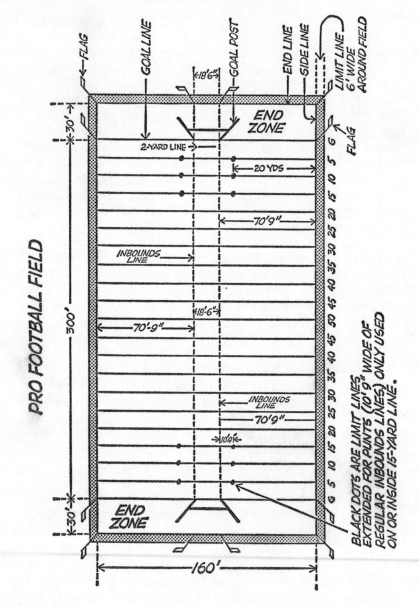

PRO FOOTBALL FIELD

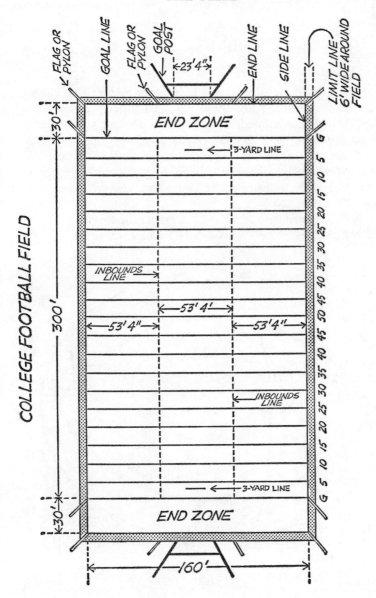

COLLEGE FOOTBALL FIELD

FLAG OR PYLON

GOAL LINE

FLAG OR PYLON

GOAL POST

←23'4"→

END LINE

SIDE LINE

LIMIT LINE 6' WIDE AROUND FIELD

30'

END ZONE

← 3-YARD LINE

INBOUNDS LINE →

← 53'4' →

← 53'4" →

← 53'4" →

← INBOUNDS LINE

300'

3-YARD LINE

END ZONE

30'

← 160' →

THE BALL

The football, for those of you who have never seen one up close, is drawn on this page. Although it has been lovingly called "the pigskin" for almost a hundred years, it is absolutely not made from the skin of a pig. The ball is made of pebble-grained leather and occasionally of rubber. The pro rules require the use of leather footballs only, while the college rules do permit a rubber-covered ball if both teams agree, but most college games are played with leather footballs.

The ball is inflated with 12½ to 13½ pounds of air.

The ball must weigh between 14 and 15 ounces.

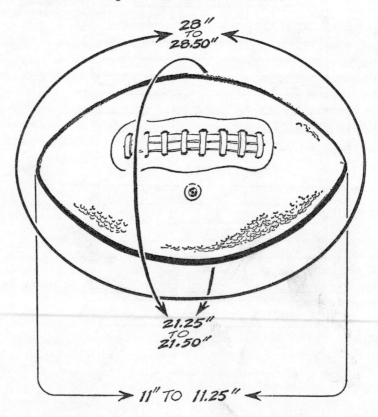

EQUIPMENT

It may be interesting to note that although a football player wears the toughest and finest equipment that money can buy, he is not actually required to wear most of it. The college rules require a player to wear the following: jersey with numbers, soft knee pads ½" thick, helmet, and fitted mouth protector.

The other obvious items are conspicuous by their absence. No pants are required by rule and no shoes either. Shoulder pads and hip pads are also omitted from the rule. It is well known that all of the above-mentioned equipment is worn during play, with the exception of an occasional bare-footed punter or place kicker.

The pro rules require a player to wear the following: jersey with numbers, pants, helmet, and stockings. The pro league makes the wearing of pants mandatory, but like the college rules, shoes are optional.

Equipment actually worn by most football players, whether they are pro or college participants, follows:

Supporter	Arm pads	Shoes
T-shirt	Hand pads	Neck pad
Hip pads	Thigh pads	Helmet with face guard
Shoulder pads	Elbow pads	Mouth protector
Rib pads	Pants	"A lot of tape"
Knee pads	Jersey	
Shin pads	Stockings	

If any equipment worn by a player is in any way dangerous to his opponents, he must replace the equipment immediately or leave the game.

THE OFFICIALS

Officials are charged with the responsibility of administering the rules of the game. To effectively fulfill this responsibility, officials must be in the most advantageous position at all times when making a call. With this in mind, "mechanics" of officiating have been developed. Just as a coach trains his players to assume a certain position on the field in any given situation, officials are trained to react to play action. They are provided with mechanics that endeavor to provide coverage prior to the snap and immediately after the snap. This is true whether it is a running play, passing play, or kicking down. Mechanics supply coverage for all game situations from the time a team comes out of the huddle until that particular play ends. Through constant study and application of current mechanics, the officials remain abreast of the constantly changing techniques employed in today's games.

Areas of concern do vary in high school, college, and pro ball; therefore mechanics, although basically similar in philosophy, will differ in the positioning of the officials. In a brief, simple explanation it may be possible to inform you as a reader of the various positions and the basic responsibilities common to that position. It will provide enough information to make you an authority on officiating on your block.

Six-man crews are used in pro ball and presently in four major college conferences. Most college games, however, are using five-man crews. The mechanics provided here are for six-man crews, since the majority of schools will be using the six men in the very near future.

PRO OFFICIATING MECHANICS

The pro game, because of their extensive use of the straight drop back technique on passes, is deeply concerned with play action downfield. Thus, because of the importance of deep coverage, they concentrate on the deeper phase of their mechanics. They maintain the strength necessary to cover the passes and the interior line play, but always remain aware of the constant pressure of deep responsibility. Officiating crews consist of a referee, umpire, head linesman, line judge, field judge, and back judge. The following diagram shows the initial position of each official on a running or passing play:

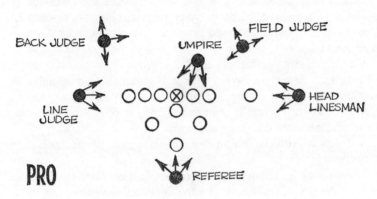

PRO OFFICIALS AND THEIR DUTIES

Referee

Charged with the control and general oversight of the game. He is the final authority when disagreement exists. May make decisions on any matter not specifically covered by the rules.

1. Responsible for conducting the toss of the coin.

2. Sounds whistle to start the game and the second half. Also puts the ball in play by blowing his whistle on any kickoff.

3. Administers the dead ball and succeeding down.

4. Must notify teams when all time outs have been used.

5. Notifies the coaches when two minutes remain in the half.

6. Administers any foul that is called by explaining the option (if any) involved and assessing penalty as prescribed by rule.

7. Observes play from any position behind any offensive backfield player, including those men in motion.

8. Primarily responsible for the quarterback. Follows behind

the play as it develops and is always alert for a change of possession, causing ball to return to his zone.

9. Responsible for measurements.

10. Rules on try-for-point kicks.

Umpire

Generally recognized as the official who controls the emotions of the game. Charged with the primary responsibility for legality of equipment and the actions and conduct of the players on the line of scrimmage.

1. Sole authority on legality of equipment.

2. Makes player inspection before the game. Also remains in charge of equipment during the game.

3. Records result of the coin toss. Keeps a record of the number of charged time outs for each team.

4. Takes a position behind the defensive line, always adjusting as necessary.

5. Responsible for the legality of blocks immediately after the snap on the line of scrimmage, by the interior linemen.

6. Watches for ineligible linemen downfield on a pass play.

7. Charged with dry ball responsibility during inclement weather. Must keep the game ball dry between downs.

8. Must be agile and "catlike" or suffer the consequences.

9. Responsible for controlling attempts by the defense to simulate starting signals of the offense. This is called signal jamming.

Head Linesman

Takes a position on the line of scrimmage and opposite the line judge. (When conditions permit, they switch field positions at the half.) He is in charge of the chain crew (two men handling stakes on either end of a ten-yard chain and one man responsible for the number of the down).

1. Primarily responsible for offside and encroachment.

2. Covers the action on the line of scrimmage by and against the men on the end of the line.

3. Responsible for any ball carrier who comes into his zone.

4. Gives forward progress to the referee.

5. Communicates the down to the referee.

6. Responsible for eligible receivers on pass plays.

7. Sideline responsibility from end line to end line.

Line Judge

Takes a position on the side of the field opposite the head lines-man and on the line of scrimmage.

1. Observes all motion in the offensive backfield.

2. Supervises timing in case the field clock breaks down. He will then take over official timing of the game.

3. Notifies the referee when the two-minute warning should be given.

4. Fires a pistol at the close of all periods.

5. Calls offside or encroachment.

6. Observes the action of players outside of umpire's vision for illegal use of hands or ineligible receivers downfield.

7. Assists the referee in ruling on false starts and forward or lateral passes.

8. Assumes responsibility for the ball carrier when play action is in his area.

9. Responsible for the sideline between his position and that of the back judge.

10. Assists the referee in determining forward progress.

11. Rules on legality of pass if line of scrimmage is threatened.

12. Times the intermission between halves.

Back Judge

Operates on the same side of the field as the line judge, thirteen to fifteen yards deep.

1. Counts the defensive players.

2. Observes all eligible players on his side of the field.

3. Observes the action of receivers between the umpire and the field judge, especially contact of linebackers with pass receivers.

4. Must help in ruling on passes that are trapped.

5. Has sideline responsibility from approximately fifteen yards beyond the line of scrimmage to the end line.

6. Rules on passes thrown deep to his sideline.

7. Covers an upright opposite the field judge on a field goal try and rules on same.

8. Rules on blocks in front of the receivers on punts.

Field Judge

Takes a position fifteen to twenty yards deep on the defensive side, favoring the head linesman's side of the field. He is responsible for the end line and therefore never permits a player to get behind him.

1. Charged with responsibility for the thirty-second count, the time a team is allowed by rule to put the ball into play.

2. Times the time outs.

3. Primarily responsible for covering action on punt receivers. He rules on the validity of a fair catch, interference with the opportunity to make a catch, and the status of the ball (touchback, safety, touchdown, etc.).

4. On pass plays he is responsible for action by or against the deep receivers.

5. Rules on legality of the kickoff tee and also informs the kicker to refrain from kicking the ball until the referee blows his whistle.

6. Assists the head linesman in the control of continuing action when he rules a ball out of bounds on his side of the field.

7. Covers an upright opposite the back judge on a field goal try and rules on same.

COLLEGE OFFICIATING MECHANICS

College rules and the various optional methods of attack now existing in college football put the major area of concern in rules administration on or within five yards of the scrimmage line. The crack back rule, protecting the quarterback and any other deep back, and illegal picks just beyond the line, caused the formulating of mechanics to cover this action. College officials carry the same titles as the pros, but they are in different positions on the field. The mechanics vary somewhat, but both groups are parallel in their philosophy and their administrative capacity. The diagram below indicates the initial position of each official on running and passing plays.

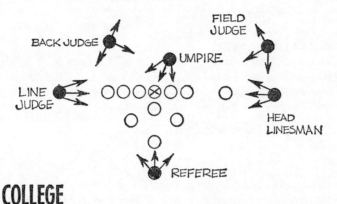

COLLEGE

Referee

As in pro ball, he is charged with the general oversight and control of the game. He is the final authority when disagreement exists. He may make decisions on any matter not specifically covered by the rules. He administers the toss of the coin prior to the game.

1. Takes a position behind the deepest back and about three yards toward the open side of the field.

2. Primarily responsible for action on the quarterback when a team employs the "wishbone" offense or any other optional formation.

3. Times the twenty-five-second count (to put the ball into play), the charged time outs, and the intermission between periods.

4. Sounds his whistle to start the game and the second half. Likewise on any kickoff following a score.

5. Must administer the necessary mechanics when the ball becomes dead and be absolutely sure the ball is put into play at the proper place for the next down.

6. Observes the offensive backs for illegal motion prior to and at the snap as well as watching for illegal shifts.

7. Must notify coaches when time outs have been exhausted.

8. Administers all fouls that are called by explaining the options and assessing the proper penalty as prescribed by rule.

9. Responsible for measurements.

10. Observes the action on passes to determine legality.

11. Provides the spot where the ball will next be put in play after a punt has gone out of bounds in flight. Directs the covering official with an arm signal.

12. Becomes the trailing or back-up official on a long gain and makes sure that no fouls occur behind the play. If a fumble or an interception should occur he becomes the deep official and will be responsible for the goal line if the interceptor or recoverer approaches the goal line.

Umpire

1. Sole authority on legality of equipment.

2. Makes player inspection before the game. Also remains in charge of equipment during the game.

3. Responsible for the proper lateral position of the ball for the next down after an incompleted forward pass.

4. Takes a position behind the defensive line, always adjusting as necessary.

5. Responsible for the legality of blocks on the line immediately after the ball is snapped. He observes both offensive and defensive players.

6. Watches for ineligible linemen downfield on a pass play.

7. Charged with dry-ball responsibility during inclement weather.

8. Must be agile and "catlike" or suffer the consequences.

9. Responsible for controlling attempts by the defense to simulate starting signals of the offense. This is called signal jamming.

Head Linesman

He positions himself on the sideline opposite the press box. He instructs the chain men and box man in their responsibilities prior to the game. He remains in charge of the chain crew throughout the game.

1. Primarily responsible for the legality of the scrimmage line, offside, illegal formation, ineligible pass receivers downfield, and illegal procedure. Also rules on the legality of a forward pass thrown when the passer is near the line of scrimmage.

2. Provides the referee with the forward progress of the runner.

3. If the play comes toward him, he observes the action of players on and behind the line of scrimmage. When the ball car-rier comes into his zone he assumes the ball-carrier responsibility while the referee, umpire, and field judge observe action in the fringe area.

4. Covers action behind the line of scrimmage when the play goes to the other side of the field. He then proceeds downfield when the ball carrier crosses the line of scrimmage.

5. Has sideline responsibility from the offensive team's end line to approximately twelve yards beyond the line of scrimmage.

6. Holds on the line of scrimmage on a pass play when the quarterback drops straight back. Assists the referee in observing pass-protection blocking.

7. Responsible for the kicker and the holder on a try for point or during an attempt at a field goal.

8. Communicates the down to the referee after a dead ball.

Line Judge

Assumes a position on the sideline opposite the head linesman.

1. Along with the head linesman, he rules primarily on the legality of the line of scrimmage, offside, illegal formation, in-eligible pass receivers downfield, and illegal procedure.

2. Informs the referee concerning the forward progress of the runner.

3. If the play comes toward him, he observes the action of players on and behind the line of scrimmage. When the ball carrier comes into his zone he assumes responsibility for the ball carrier while the referee, umpire, and back judge observe action in the fringe area.

4. Covers action behind the line of scrimmage when the play goes to the other side of the field. He then proceeds downfield when the ball carrier crosses the line of scrimmage.

5. Normally has sideline responsibility for his whole sideline. The exception is on an option pass when the play comes in his direction; he then covers only fifteen yards beyond the line of scrimmage.

6. On straight drop-back pass he will flow approximately ten yards downfield and observe the action from that spot. Has side-line responsibility from end line to end line.

7. Rules on the blocking action of the receiver of a punt. If the receiver makes a fair-catch signal, the line judge is responsible for seeing that the receiver making the signal does not block a member of the kicking team.

Field Judge

Operates on the same side of the field as the head linesman, twelve to fifteen yards deep.

1. Observes the action of receivers coming downfield on his side of the field.

2. Watches for legality of crack back blocks and "picks."

3. Has sideline responsibility from fifteen yards beyond the line of scrimmage to the end line.

4. Helps on ruling of passes that are trapped.

5. Has deep pass responsibility on his side of the field.

6. Covers one upright while the back judge covers the other on all field-goal and extra-point attempts. They both decide whether the kick is good or not good.

7. Observes the receiving team's blocks in front of a punt receiver. He must also be alert to the action of a man signaling for a fair catch and not catching the ball. This player is restricted from any blocking during the rest of the down.

8. Covers continuing action beyond the sideline when the head linesman marks the out-of-bounds spot.

Back Judge

Takes a position fifteen to twenty yards deep favoring the side of the line judge. He has end line responsibility; therefore he must never permit a player to get behind him.

1. Primarily responsible for deep action on punt receiver and pass receiver.

2. Rules on the validity of the fair catch, interference with the opportunity to catch a punt, the status of the ball after punted (e.g., touchback, safety), and follows the advance of the receiver until he moves into the area of another official. He then covers the action in the fringe area.

3. Rules on pass interference in his area.

4. Observes the legality of crack back blocks on his side of the field.

5. Rules on the legality of the kickoff.

6. Covers one upright while the field judge covers the other on all field-goal and extra-point attempts. They both decide whether the kick is good or not good.

Hopefully this will provide an insight into the positions and some of the responsibilities of the officials. To completely cover the mechanics would require writing another book. The information provided, however, will at least provide you with the knowledge of who is to blame when an official fails to cover a play.

FOULS AND PENALTIES

Football rules have been formulated over the years to control the game. These rules deny the players the opportunity to employ tactics that would give them an unfair advantage during play. They also provide for the safety of the participants. The infractions carry different penalties depending upon the severity of the action by the player or the team. It should be apparent that the structure of football rules is very similar to the rules of everyday life. The difference is in the administration. A court case may involve an arresting officer, an attorney, and in some cases a judge and a jury. In football the official is all of these in one. Whereas it sometimes takes hours, weeks, months, or even years to settle a civil or criminal case, an official must enforce the rules instantaneously. This may be one valid reason why he is so unpopular with the average fan. Finally, it must be pointed out that penalties against a team may always be declined by their opponents, if they choose to do so.

In the next few pages you will find most of the pro and college fouls and the penalties that they carry. Many fouls are the same in both codes and an almost equal number are different.

SUMMARY OF PENALTIES
(*Professional*)

Loss of Down

1. Making second forward pass from behind scrimmage line.

2. When a forward pass touches a second eligible offensive man or an ineligible offensive man behind the line of scrimmage.

3. Pass that hits ground, crossbar, or goal post or goes out of bounds.

4. Second eligible pass receiver catching pass.

5. Passers catching second forward pass.

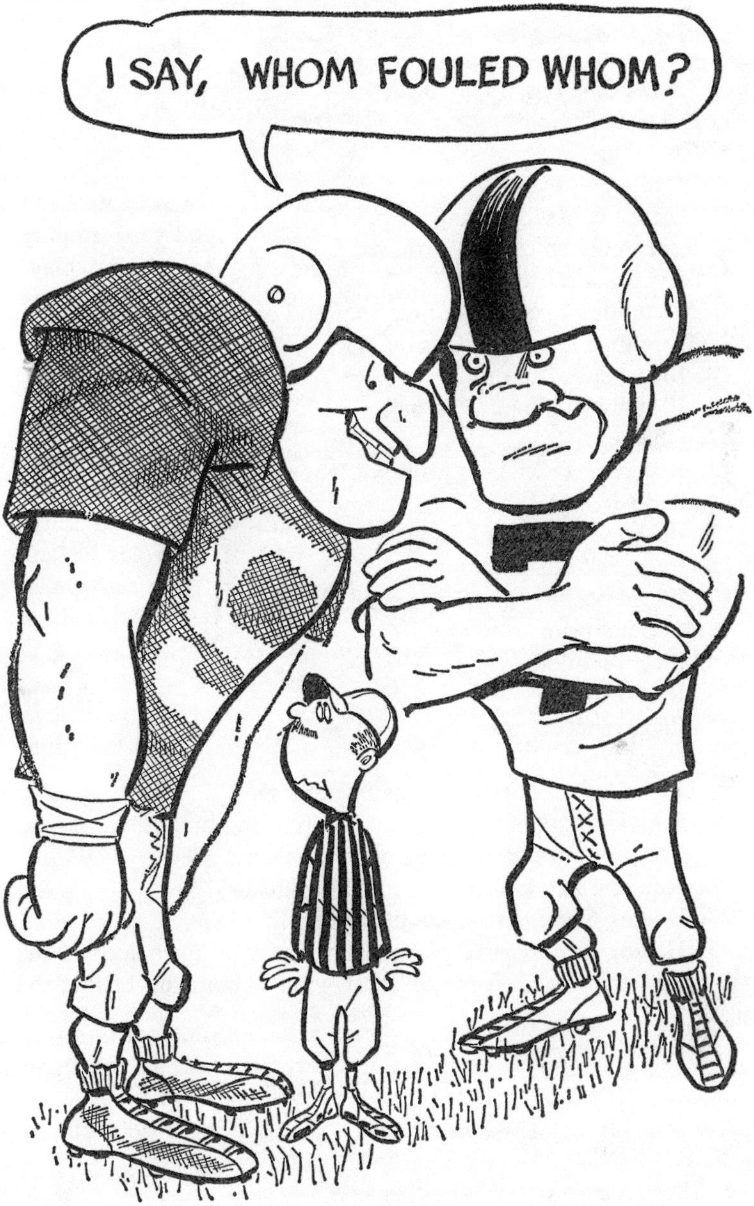
I SAY, WHOM FOULED WHOM?

Loss of Five Yards

1. Excess time out.
2. Delay of game.
3. Crawling.
4. Illegal equipment.
5. Defense contacting snapper or ball.
6. Repeatedly entering neutral zone.
7. Advance after fair catch.
8. Attempting to conserve time near end of period.
9. More than eleven players on field.
10. Illegal substitution.
11. Illegally kicking at free ball.
12. Offside.
13. Receiving or kicking team not inbounds on free kick.
14. Short free kick.
15. Illegal touching of free kick.
16. Free kick out of bounds.
17. Illegal position of offense at snap.
18. Contact prior to snap.
19. Illegal motion.
20. Illegal shift.
21. Illegal snap.
22. False start.
23. Illegal use of hands or arms by defense.
24. Forward pass in field of play not from scrimmage.
25. Forward pass beyond line of scrimmage.
26. Running into kicker (not roughing kicker).
27. Having fewer than seven players on line.
28. Having an offensive player who is not within a foot of the ball at the snap or who is not a full yard behind the ball at the snap.
29. Illegally locking legs on line.

Loss of Fifteen Yards

1. Illegal delay at start of either half.
2. Pass interference by offense.

3. Fair-catch interference. Also loss of ball.

4. Roughing the maker of a fair catch.

5. Runner grabbing or holding a teammate.

6. Interlocking interference.

7. Illegal use of hands or arms by offense.

8. Illegal batting or punching the ball.

9. Kicking or kicking at the ball except legal kick.

10. Striking opponent.

11. Kneeing opponent.

12. Kicking opponent.

13. Roughing the kicker.

14. Piling.

15. Hurdling.

16. Tripping.

17. Striking opponent above knee with foot or shin.

18. Charging into opponent who is out of bounds.

19. Charging into player obviously out of play.

20. Clipping.

21. Roughing the passer.

22. Committing any unnecessary roughness.

23. Abusive language by players.

24. Disconcerting signals.

25. Concealing the ball.

26. Abusing officials.

27. Violating substitution rule to conserve time.

28. Violating thirty-second rule more than twice during same down.

29. Player on field communicating to someone other than the coach.

30. Team representatives using unsportsmanlike conduct.

31. Nonplayers going on field.

32. Nonplayers moving along sideline.

Loss of Half the Distance to the Goal Line

1. Pass interference by defense in their own end zone with spot of the previous snap being inside the one-yard line.

2. Distance of penalty exceeds half the distance to either goal line.

Loss of Ball

1. Failure to make first down.

2. Kicking team first touching a kick in the field of play except kickoff.

3. Interfering with fair catch. Also a 15-yard penalty.

Penalties Resulting in First Down

1. Defense foul during a play from scrimmage gives the offense an automatic first down, with the following exceptions:

A. Excess time out.

B. Delay of game.

C. Illegal substitution.

D. Illegal equipment.

E. Offside.

F. False start.

G. Defense touching the center.

2. Defensive pass interference.

SUMMARY OF PENALTIES
(*Collegiate*)

Loss of a Down

1. Illegally handling the ball forward (also loss of five yards).

2. Intentionally throwing a backward pass out of bounds (also loss of five yards).

3. Illegal forward pass by the offensive team (also loss of five yards).

4. Intentionally grounding a forward pass (also loss of five yards).

5. Forward pass illegally touched by an originally eligible pass receiver beyond the line (he becomes ineligible by going out of bounds).

6. Offensive pass interference (also loss of fifteen yards).

7. Forward pass illegally touched behind neutral zone by an ineligible receiver (also loss of five yards).

8. Forward pass illegally touched beyond neutral zone by an ineligible receiver (also loss of fifteen yards).

Loss of Five Yards

1. Improper numbering of players.

2. Excess time out illegally used or requested by a team.

3. Illegal delay of game by either team.

4. Crawling or trying to advance a dead ball.

5. Unfair tactics such as trying to consume time illegally.

6. Infraction of the substitution rules.

7. Putting the ball in play before the ball is declared ready for play.

8. Exceeding the twenty-five-second count.

9. Infraction of the free kick formation.

10. Player out of bounds when the ball is free kicked (offense or defense).

11. Free kick out of bounds untouched by an inbounds receiver.

12. Illegal kick.

13. Taking more than two steps after fair catch is completed.

14. Illegal snap of the ball by the center.

15. More than one ball adjustment by snapper.

16. All members of the offensive team not within fifteen yards of the ball after ready-for-play signal is given.

17. False start or simulating start of play by the offensive team.

18. Interference with opponents or ball.

19. Infraction of scrimmage formation.

20. Offensive or defensive offside.

21. Offensive player out of bounds when the ball is snapped.

22. Offensive player illegally in motion at the snap.

23. Player on the scrimmage line receiving the snap from center.

24. Failure to pause one full second after a shift.

25. Illegally handling the ball forward (also loss of down if by the offensive team).

26. Intentionally throwing backward pass out of bounds (also loss of down if by the offensive team).

27. Illegal forward pass (also loss of down if by the offensive team).

28. Intentionally grounding of a forward pass (also loss of the down).

29. Forward pass illegally touched by ineligible receiver behind neutral zone (also loss of down).

30. Interlocked interference or helping the runner.

Loss of Fifteen Yards

1. Illegally batting of a forward pass in flight.

2. Illegal equipment used during play.

3. Illegal sideline conference with coach or coaches.

4. Team not ready to play at the start of either half.

5. Interference with the opportunity to catch a kick.

6. Invalid signal for a fair catch.

7. Block by the fair-catch signaler.

8. Tackling or blocking a fair catcher.

9. Offensive pass interference (also loss of down).

10. Ineligible receiver downfield.

11. Forward pass illegally touched beyond the neutral zone (also loss of down).

12. Striking, kicking, kneeing, elbowing, etc.

13. Meeting with the knee, striking with the open hand, etc.

14. Tripping, blocking below waist.

15. Clipping.

16. Piling on.

17. Tackling out of bounds after the ball is dead.

18. Hurdling.

19. Grabbing face mask of opponent.

20. Butting—helmet or head spearing.

21. Roughing the kicker or holder.

22. Substitute interference.

23. Blocking below the waist.

24. Abusive or insulting language.

25. Defensive disconcerting signals.

26. Persons illegally on field.

27. Player not returning the ball directly to an official after a play ends.

28. Unsportsmanlike conduct.

29. Persons other than team players entering playing field.

30. Concealing the ball from opponents.

31. Illegal return of a disqualified player.

32. Illegal use of hand or arm by the offense.

33. Illegal use of hand or arm by the defense.

34. Illegally kicking the ball by either team.

35. Foul before a scrimmage kick or free kick is touched.

Loss of Half the Distance to the Goal Line

1. Foul by the defensive team behind its own goal line when the enforcement spot is inside the one-yard line.

2. If the distance of the penalty exceeds half the distance to either goal line.

Offended Team's Ball at the Spot of the Foul

1. Defensive pass interference.

2. Illegal use of hand or arm when the ball is free.

3. Illegally batting a free ball.

4. Illegally kicking a free ball.

Violation (Not a Foul)

1. Illegal touching of a free kick by the kicking team.

2. Illegal touching of a scrimmage kick by the kicking team.

TIMING AND SUBSTITUTIONS

I wonder how many of you football fans have ever seen a "sleeper" play. Probably very few, because I have only seen two in my seventeen years of officiating. My first "sleeper" came in a game between Podunk University and some other small college. Podunk was losing by three points with very little time remaining in the game. Podunk had the ball and, on second down, ran an end sweep to about their own forty-yard line. The runner was a little slow getting up and it looked like he was hurt on the play. He removed his helmet and started toward the sideline just like any replaced player would do. The defensive players paid no attention to him as he trotted "off" the field.

Podunk rushed to the line of scrimmage and our "replaced player" quickly put his helmet on and set for the required one second with the rest of his team. The ball was snapped and the "sleeper" streaked down the sideline. He caught a perfect pass around the twenty-five-yard line and scored the winning touchdown, with the nearest defender twenty-five yards upfield. Podunk had completely faked their opponents out with an illegal "sleeper" play. They also faked out the officials. Were we embarrassed!

My second "sleeper" play came in a high school game on the opening play from scrimmage after the kickoff. The receiving team started the game with ten men, which is perfectly legal. As soon as the ball was blown dead, one player ran off the field and a replacement came on. The defensive team naturally assumed that the receivers had started the game with eleven men, so when one man left and one came in, how were they to know that the team with the ball still had only ten men on the field?

The play was called, and just before the snap the eleventh man stepped from the sideline and raced downfield unattended. He caught a pass for a touchdown, but the officials called the play back.

"Sleeper" plays are illegal in pro, college, and high school football. There are hundreds of variations, but the purpose of all "sleepers" is to deceive or confuse the opposition. Keep watching; you may see one someday.

How many time outs are allowed in college and pro football?

In both college and pro ball a team is permitted three charged team time outs in each half.

Is an injury time out charged to a team?

An injury time out is charged to the referee in college and pro ball, with one exception under pro rules. If the injury occurs during the

last two minutes of either half and all time outs have been used, the referee will charge himself for the injury, but all other injury time outs during the last two minutes will cost the team with the injury a five-yard penalty.

Can a team call consecutive charged team time outs?

College and pro ball both prohibit consecutive charged team time outs.

Is there a maximum amount of time allowed for an injury time out?

There is no limit on an injury time out. Naturally, the injured man or men are removed from the field as quickly as possible.

What is the length of a charged team time out?

In college ball a charged team time out is 1½ minutes in length. Pro ball permits 2 minutes for their charged team time outs.

May any player on the field call a charged team time out?

In college ball, unless a specific captain has been designated prior to the game, any player on the field is permitted to call a time out. A player coming onto the field of play must be within fifteen yards of the ball before his request may be granted. In pro ball only a designated captain is permitted to call a time out.

Is it permissible for a player to request a time out by using a hand signal, or must this request be verbal?

There is no documented hand signal for a time-out request; however, a simulated "T" hand signal has been more or less acceptable. Rules "demand" a verbal request for a time out.

On a charged team time out, is it permissible for a team to go to the sideline for coaches' instructions?

In college ball only one player at a time is permitted to confer with the coaches. In pro ball any number of players may confer at the sideline.

Who has the responsibility for timing the time outs?

In college ball the referee is charged with this responsibility. Pro ball gives this responsibility to the field judge.

How would you define consecutive charged team time outs, and are they legal?

Under college rules consecutive charged time outs are illegal. Granting two time outs to the same team without at least one play between time outs is considered consecutive. Pro rules go a step farther. They do not permit two time outs in a row by opposing teams or the same team.

Can a team get an extra time out by taking a five-yard penalty?

It is not possible to get an additional time out by taking a five-yard penalty. Both college and pro rules prohibit this.

Who is responsible for calling television time outs?

In both college and pro ball the television network has a liaison man on the sideline who signals to the game officials when the network wants a commercial. It is up to the referee to actually call the time out.

What if a commercial is called for by the television people and one team is driving for a score?

The final decision on television time outs lies with the referee, and he will never do anything to stop the momentum of a team's drive. The commercial will just have to wait.

What do the teams do during television time outs?

The same thing they do during a charged time out. Relax a little and get instructions from the coach.

How long is a TV time out?

The commercial is generally 60 seconds in length. Officials and announcers make every effort to return to play with a minimum amount of delay following a time out for a commercial. These time outs seldom exceed 1½ minutes.

Why does the referee wind his arms around in a circle as he blows the whistle at the start of some plays, and then he will only blow the whistle and omit the winding motion on other plays?

The winding motion tells the clock operator or official timer that the clock should start. Omitting this signal means that the clock should start at the snap of the ball or that the clock never stopped and should be kept running.

How much time does a team have to put the ball into play after the referee blows his whistle, and who is responsible for keeping this time?

In college ball the offensive team gets twenty-five seconds to put the ball in play, and the time is kept by the referee. In pro ball the offensive team gets thirty seconds to put the ball in play, and this time is kept by the field judge.

Is it true that a team may tell the referee that it wants a time out after the next play and that the referee will give it to them as soon as the play is over without the customary request?

The only way a college or pro team can call a time out is to request the time out at the conclusion of a play.

What is the total playing time of a college or pro football game?

The college and pro games are the exact same length of time. Both are sixty minutes, divided into four fifteen-minute periods.

How much time is allowed between periods and halves of a football game?

Both college and pro ball allow a twenty-minute halftime. College ball allows one minute between periods, while pro ball allows two minutes between periods.

Who times the interval between periods and halves?

In college ball the referee times the one minute between periods, and the back judge times the halftime interval. In pro ball the field judge times the period interval, and the halftime intermission is timed by the line judge.

Who is the keeper of the official game clock in pro and college games?

In college ball there is an official timekeeper who operates the scoreboard clock, usually from the press box. In pro ball the official timer is generally on the sideline, and he operates the scoreboard clock from there. In both cases the scoreboard clock is the official time.

Who keeps the official game time if the scoreboard clock fails to operate?

In college ball the back judge picks up the time on a special watch that he carries for just such emergencies. In pro ball the line judge does the same job.

What is the two-minute warning?

The two-minute warning is the official notification from the referee to the head coach of each team that exactly two minutes remain in the half or the game. Only the pro league has a two-minute warning. College ball has a four-minute warning, but only if the scoreboard clock is not being used.

Does the official game clock run on a try for point?

The try for point, or "extra point," as it is often called, is always an untimed down. The clock never runs during an untimed down. College and pro rules are the same in this case.

What stops the official game clock other than an official's time out or a charged team time out?

The game clock stops when:
1. The ball or a player with the ball in possession goes out of bounds.
2. A forward pass is incomplete.
3. The ball is declared dead on a down during which a foul occurs.
4. A touchdown has been scored.
5. A field goal or safety is scored.
6. A foul occurs prior to the snap if the clock was running.
7. The offensive team makes a first down (college ball).
8. The period ends.
9. Any time the referee feels there will be an extended delay in getting the ball into play.
10. The whistle is blown after a snap or free kick.

When is a team entitled to another down when time has expired at the end of a quarter, half, or the game?

The rule is basically the same in college and pro ball. When the defensive team commits a foul during the last play of a quarter, the half, or the game, the offensive team is entitled to an untimed down, which is free of such fouls if the penalty is accepted.

A foul by the defense after the play ends is different under pro and college rules. In college ball the quarter, half, or game ends. In pro ball, if the foul is considered continuing action of the play, the quarter, half, or game is extended.

In college ball, if the offensive team fouls on the last play, the quarter, half, or game ends. It also ends in pro ball unless an offensive foul on the last play is followed by a possession change. Only then can the game be extended.

On the last play of a football game, the offensive team scores a touchdown but they are offside. Is the down replayed?

The game is over and the touchdown does not count. An offensive foul on the last play of the game ends the game.

The offensive team attempts a field goal on the last play of the half. The kick is short but the defensive team is called for an illegal use of the hands foul. What is the ruling?

The penalty is enforced and the kicking team is given an untimed down.

If a touchdown is scored on the last play of the game and no foul occurs, is the try for point allowed?

Because the try for point is always an untimed down it is always allowed after a touchdown, even if the time has expired.

Why do teams change goals at the end of the first and third periods?

This rule assures that each team will get the same amount of time with the wind at their backs. When this change takes place, team position, number of the next down, field position, and yardage to gain for a first down remain unchanged.

Is the toss of the coin always held just before the kickoff?

In college ball it is usually held at midfield three to five minutes before the kickoff. In pro ball the toss is held thirty minutes before the kickoff at midfield. A simulated toss is then held just a minute or two before the kickoff.

Why do they fire a pistol at the end of each period?

The pistol is fired as a signal to all concerned that time has expired and the period is over. The pistol will not be fired until the ball is dead at the end of the last play in the period. The line judge has this responsibility in pro ball. College ball does not use the pistol.

What happens if a football game ends in a tie?

College games remain ties and the game is over. Pro games, during regular-season play, also remain ties. During playoff and championship games a sudden-death system is employed.

How does the "sudden death" system work in pro ball?

Under this system, the team scoring first during overtime play is the winner of the game. Any score will do, including a safety or an awarded touchdown because of an unfair act.

At the end of regulation play, the referee will immediately hold another toss of the coin at midfield, with the visiting team calling the toss. Following a three-minute intermission, the game will be continued in fifteen-minute periods, with a two-minute intermission between each overtime period.

There will be no intermission as at halftime, only the two-minute break. If at the end of the fourth overtime period the score is still tied, a new toss of the coin will be held with the visitors again calling the toss if they are still able to walk out to midfield.

How much of a warning is given to the teams before the halftime intermission is over?

In both college and pro ball, the teams are warned with five minutes remaining in the halftime intermission. The field judge in college ball and line judge in pro ball are the officials who go to the team dressing rooms.

Does the clock stop if an official accidentally blows his whistle while the ball is in play?

The clock stops and the ball becomes dead even though the whistle should never have been blown. It is a situation that rarely happens, but it is thoroughly covered in both college and pro rules.

If a forward pass is in the air when an official accidentally blows his whistle, what happens to the ball?

The ball is dead as soon as the whistle blows in both pro and college ball. In pro ball, the ball is returned to the line of scrimmage and the down is counted just as if the pass were incomplete. In college ball, the down is replayed from the previous line of scrimmage and the down does not count.

What happens if an official accidentally blows his whistle while a fumble or backward pass is free on the ground?

In pro ball, the ball is given to the offensive or fumbling team at the spot of the ball when the whistle blew. In college ball, the ball is given to the fumbling team at the spot of the fumble.

If a whistle is accidentally blown while a runner is in the clear, what is the ruling?

In both pro and college ball, the ball is dead at the spot of the ball when the whistle was blown.

If a whistle is accidentally blown while a kick is in flight, what is the ruling?

In pro ball, it is the receiver's ball at the spot where the ball is when the whistle is blown. In college ball the down is replayed.

The crowd noise is so loud that the offensive players cannot hear the quarterback calling out his signals. Must the offensive team call a time out, or is this situation covered in the rules?

In pro ball the offensive quarterback would hold both hands above his head for quiet. If the crowd did not respond to this plea, the referee would stop the clock and charge himself with an official's time out. When the teams are ready and the crowd had quieted down, the clock would be started. In college ball the quarterback appeals to the referee and the clock is stopped. If the noise continues, the clock will not start until the ball is snapped even if it had been running when the official's time out was initiated.

SUBSTITUTIONS

When may a substitute come into the game?

In both college and pro ball, a legal substitute may enter the game at any time while the ball is dead. This means that substitutes can enter between periods, after a score or a try for point, or during the interval between downs.

Must an incoming substitute report to an official?

Incoming substitutes do not have to report to an official. This is the same in college and pro ball.

Can a replaced player leave the field on his opponents' side of the field?

Replaced players must leave the field on their own side of the field. Failing to do so incurs a five-yard penalty.

If the referee calls an official's time out, can substitutes come into the game?

Substitutes can come into the game any time the ball is not in play in both pro and college ball.

Don't college officials wear red-and-green armbands so that substitutes will know to whom to report?

They did during the past several football seasons, but collegiate football has now adopted a free substitution rule just like the pros.

Does a replaced player have to clear the field of play if he is clearly out of the way of all action when the ball is snapped?

Replaced players must be clearly off the field before the ball is snapped or free-kicked.

When does a substitute become a player according to rule?

In college ball a substitute becomes a player when the ball is snapped. In pro ball a substitute becomes a player when he informs a teammate that he is replacing him.

When is a player legally in the game?

A player is legally in the game when he has participated in at least one play. A player is legally substituted for when he leaves the game for at least one play.

Is there any limit on the number of substitutes allowed to enter the game when the ball is not in play?

Each team may send from one to eleven substitutes into the game after each play. College and pro ball have unlimited substitutions.

What is free substitution?

Free substitution means that either team may replace any number of players at any time when it is legal by rule to substitute.

Is it legal for a team to play with less than eleven players on the field?

In college ball the offensive team is required to have at least seven men on the line of scrimmage at the snap. They could legally play with seven men, but with no backs they would be at a slight disadvantage. The defense can play with any number from zero to eleven. On kickoffs the kickers have no minimum number of men required by rule, but on a normal kickoff the receivers must have at least five men between their own 45- and 50-yard line when it is kicked. The receiving team could legally receive a kickoff with only five men on the field. Pro rules are the same as for college on scrimmage plays. The offense must have seven men and the defense any number between zero and eleven. On kickoffs the kickers and receivers may have from zero to eleven players.

A player leaves the field of play at the end of the first period, and without a play being run, returns for the start of the second period. Isn't this an illegal substitution?

A replaced player must stay out of the game for one play unless the period ends when he leaves. The period ending is considered the same as a play. The player is legally in the game in both college and pro ball.

Is it a foul if a substitute enters the field of play and communicates with a teammate and then leaves the field without participating in one play?

In college ball it is not a foul. A substitute may enter and leave again before the snap or free kick. In pro ball it is an unsportsmanlike conduct foul.

Twelve men are discovered on the field for either team at the end of a down. What is the penalty?

In both college and pro ball it is an unsportsmanlike conduct foul, and it carries a fifteen-yard penalty. Even if it is not certain that this man actually participated in the play, the penalty is enforced. The rules consider this illegal participation.

An offensive man is running in the clear for what looks like a sure touchdown when a substitute dashes from the bench and tackles the runner. What is the ruling?

In college ball if the official felt that the runner would have scored, the touchdown is awarded to the offended team. In pro ball the official may enforce any distance penalty that he considers equitable.

A replaced player has not reached the sideline when the offensive team is called for delay of game. What is the ruling?

In pro and college ball the replaced player is not affected and he continues off of the field. The only penalty assessed is five yards for delay of game against the offensive team.

A replaced defensive player leaves the field on the opponents' side and then a delay of game penalty is called against the offensive team. Is this a foul?

In both college and pro ball it is a foul by the replaced player. The moment he reaches the wrong sideline he has fouled. The delay of game penalty would become part of a double foul. A double foul occurs when both teams foul during a down or during the dead-ball period, as in the above situation. The fouls in this case would offset each other.

Can a coach use incoming substitutes to send in plays from the sideline?

You see it done all of the time. Both college and pro coaches often send in plays with substitutes. Some coaches have two offensive men who actually alternate on every play so that the coach can call each offensive play of the game and not have to use too many substitutes.

Can a substitute call a time out as he is running onto the field?

In college ball he must be within fifteen yards of the football in order to legally call a time out. If he is not within fifteen yards the request for a time out is not recognized by the officials. In pro ball the request for a time out by an incoming substitute is not allowed unless the field captain's request is granted before the ball is put into play.

Is there any limit on the number of times a man can go into and out of the game?

In both pro and college ball a man can become a player and a substitute an unlimited number of times during a game.

KICKOFF

An onside or short kickoff is an attempt by the kicking team to recover a short kick after it has traveled the required ten yards or after it has touched a member of the receiving team. It is a dangerous play and is usually used when time is running out and the kicking team is behind.

In pro ball, if the ball is touched or recovered by the kickers before it travels the ten yards or before it is touched by the receiver, it is a foul; the kickers are penalized five yards, and the ball is kicked again.

In college ball a recovery or a touching by the kickers before the ball has traveled ten yards is a violation, and at the end of the down the receivers can take the ball at the spot of the illegal touching by the kicking team. In both college and pro ball, once the ball travels ten yards it's anybody's ball to recover, but only the receiver can advance the ball.

The Dallas Cowboys were trailing the San Francisco 49ers 28–13 in a recent playoff game with ten minutes left to play. A Dallas drive was stopped around midfield and they settled for a field goal, making the score 28–16. Things looked bad for the Cowboys.

The two-minute warning was given with Dallas in possession on their own forty-five-yard line. Only two minutes left to play and they needed two touchdowns to win. Impossible! Three great passes and a successful extra point made the score 28–23. The clock showed ninety seconds left to play.

It was quite obvious that Dallas would try an onside kick in an attempt to regain possession of the ball. The odds were definitely not in their favor. They had just moved fifty-five yards in thirty seconds, and how much "luck" could a team have in a clutch situation like this? The kicker approached the ball and it bounded crazily downfield. It traveled the required ten yards, and after a

mad scramble for the elusive "pigskin," Dallas miraculously recovered the ball at the fifty-yard line.

The game clock showed eighty-eight seconds to play, and Dallas drove the fifty yards to a score in just thirty-six seconds. The
extra point made the final score Dallas 30, San Francisco 28. The
onside kick had done its job once again.

**How does a football game begin? Everyone knows the answer to
that. Or do they?**

First of all, there is the pregame ritual called "the toss of the
coin." It is exactly that, a toss of a coin to determine which team
will kick, receive, or defend what goal. The team that wins the
toss gets to pick one of the three choices. The loser obviously gets
a choice of what remains. The referee then signals the results of
the toss to the press and the crowd. The teams line up, and after a
signal from the referee, the kicking team kicks off, which is the one
and only way a football game can begin.

With the kicking team ready to kick off, the kicker, in his attempt to kick the ball, misses it completely. A receiving team man grabs the ball from the kicking tee and runs for a touchdown. Is this legal?

It is illegal because, according to rule, the game cannot start until the ball is kicked. In this case, the game hasn't started.

The ball is blown off the kicking tee just before the kicker arrives at the ball. Can he kick the ball from the ground?

If the ball is blown behind the kicker's line it may be kicked without penalty. If it is blown beyond the kicker's line it may also be kicked, but it will be a five-yard penalty against the kicking team.

Must the kicking tee be made of some special material?

The kicking tee may be made of any material as long as it does not exceed the height requirement of the league. The tee can even be made from the soil in the general vicinity of the spot where the ball will be kicked.

Can a tee be used on all place kicks during a football game?

In college ball, a tee can be used on all place kicks. In pro ball a tee can be used on kickoffs only.

Is it mandatory that a kicking tee be used on a kickoff?

No. However, if one is used it can be no higher than three inches above the ground in pro ball and two inches in the college game.

When can a member of the kicking team legally recover his own kickoff?

The ball can legally be recovered after it has traveled ten yards or as soon as it has touched any member of the receiving team, even if the touching occurs before the ball travels the ten yards.

May the kicking team catch or recover their own kick and advance it?

The kicking team can never advance their own kick. (A kicked ball continues to be a kick until it is caught, blown dead by an official, or goes out of bounds.) However, a team member may catch his team's kick providing there is no member of the receiving team in a position to make the catch.

The ball is kicked off on a low trajectory, resulting in a line-drive kick that hits a member of the receiving team in the chest and rebounds into the hands of the kicker, who runs for a touchdown. Is this legal?

Absolutely not. It is the kicking team's ball at the spot of recovery. The instant the kicking team gains possession of their own kick it is dead by rule.

A kickoff goes only seven yards and is recovered by the kicking team. It is not touched by the receivers. Who gets the ball?

In college ball the receivers are given the ball at the spot of recovery. Under pro rules the kicking team is penalized five yards and the ball is kicked again.

Is a kickoff out of bounds an automatic penalty in both college and pro ball?

In pro ball it is an automatic five-yard penalty and the ball is kicked again. In college ball the receiving team has the option of putting the ball in play at the inbounds line where it went out of bounds or of taking a five-yard penalty against the kicking team and a rekick.

A kickoff is touched by a member of the kicking team and then rolls out of bounds without being touched by a member of the receiving team. Is this a foul?

It sure is! In pro ball it is a five-yard penalty and the ball is rekicked. In college ball it is a five-yard penalty and the ball is rekicked, or the receivers can have the ball where it went out of bounds.

A kickoff is touched by a receiving team man and then goes out of bounds. Is this a foul?

It is not a foul whenever a receiver touches a kickoff before it goes out of bounds. They must, however, put the ball in play at the inbounds line where the ball went out of bounds.

A member of the kicking team is blocked out of bounds on the kickoff and then returns to recover the ball after it has touched the leg of a man of the receiving team. The kick recovery is made on the kicking team's forty-eight-yard line. Is it a legal recovery even though the ball only traveled eight yards?

In college ball the recovery is legal. Once a player on the receiving team touches a kickoff it becomes a free ball and anyone can recover, even if the player making the recovery had gone out of bounds. In pro ball, once the man on the kicking team goes out of bounds, he is restricted from touching or recovering the ball until it has been possessed by the receivers.

How close to the ball can a receiving team line up on a kickoff?

Ordinarily the kick is made from the kicker's forty-yard line and the receiving team may not be any closer than the fifty-yard line. The distance is always ten yards between restraining lines, regardless of the yard line from which the kick is made.

The receiving team's deep receivers are out of bounds in the end zone as the ball is kicked. Is this legal?

It is illegal. All receivers and kickers must be inbounds on the playing field when the ball is kicked for a kickoff.

On the kickoff, the ball passes through the uprights. Will the kicking team be awarded three points?

In college or pro ball the kick would not score a field goal.

A kickoff hits a goal post and is then caught by a receiver. Is this ball in play?

In both pro and college ball the ball is automatically dead and the play is an automatic touchback.

A kickoff goes into the end zone where it is caught and advanced by a receiver who bumps into the goal post. Does this have any effect on the play?

In pro ball the goal posts are on the goal line and any contact with the post by a player is ignored. The bumping has no effect on the play according to rule, but it might slow him down a bit.

In college ball the goal posts are on the end line, and if a player with the ball bumps the post he is out of bounds.

A kickoff, while in flight, hits a member of the receiving team positioned in his end zone. It is subsequently caught or recovered in the end zone by a member of the kicking team. What is the ruling?

It is a touchdown for the kicking team in both pro and college ball.

A kickoff bounces into the receivers' end zone where it is recovered by the kicking team. What is the ruling?

It is a touchdown in pro ball, but it is an automatic touchback in college ball. Under college rules any kickoff that strikes the ground in the receiving team's end zone untouched by any member of the receiving team is a touchback. The pros have no such rule, and any ball going into the receiver's end zone is free and can be recovered by either team.

Does the game clock start at the beginning of a game, or whenever there is a kickoff?

In college ball the clock starts when the ball is legally touched by either team. In pro ball the clock starts when the ball is kicked, except during the last two minutes of each half. Then it is the same as the college rule.

Can a forward pass be made on a kickoff?

Absolutely not! No forward passes can be made after possession changes. The only passes that are legal on a kickoff are backward and lateral passes.

A kickoff into a stiff wind comes down behind the spot from where the kick was made, and a receiver picks it up and runs for a touchdown. Is this legal?

The touchdown is legal. The receiving team can always run with a kicked ball. The kicking team could only have recovered the ball.

Can you punt the ball on a kickoff?

A punt is only legal on a kickoff after a safety has been scored. On all other kickoffs the ball must be drop kicked or place kicked.

A kickoff rolls dead on the receiving team's five-yard line, where it is blown dead by an official. No one makes any attempt to recover the ball. Who gets it?

The ball belongs to the receiving team. Whenever a kicked ball is declared dead in possession of neither team, it is awarded to the receiving team at the spot where the ball was blown dead.

What is a squib kick?

It is a kick in which the kicker intentionally applies a technique that causes the ball to roll crazily along the playing surface. The resulting unpredictable bounces make it difficult for the receiving team to gain possession. This kick can be made from a kicking tee or directly from the playing surface.

A man on the receiving team is blocked into a kickoff that has gone only eight yards, and the ball hits him in the leg. The kicking team recovers. Is this a legal recovery?

The forced touching is ignored. Under pro rules this play would be ruled a short free kick and a five-yard penalty. Under collegiate rules the ball would be awarded to the receivers at the spot of the recovery.

A kickoff is caught by a deep receiver on his five-yard line, and he breaks into the clear. At the fifty-yard line he falls to the ground without any contact from the other team. Is the play over?

In pro ball the runner can get up and go again. He is not considered down unless contact by an opponent caused him to fall to the turf. Under college rules the receiver would be down even if a slip caused contact with the ground.

A kickoff is caught in the end zone, and the receiver runs back and forth without ever getting out of the end zone. He is finally tackled. Is it a safety or a touchback?

A touchback. It might appear to be a safety, but the ball was put into the end zone by a kick, and as long as the runner remains in the end zone it is a touchback. It is the receivers' ball, first and ten at the twenty-yard line.

Can a fair catch signal be given legally on a kickoff?

It is legal to fair catch a kickoff, and the receiver who signals is protected from being hit by his opponents if he makes the catch. However, he is denied the privilege of advancing.

A man on the receiving team signals for a fair catch of a kickoff and successfully makes the catch on his own forty-eight-yard line. Does he have the option of trying a free-kick field goal, or does he have to put the ball in play with a snap from the center?

In college ball the receiving team must put the ball in play with a snap. They have no chance to free kick. In pro ball if a fair catch is made, the receiving team has the option of putting the ball in play by a regular snap from center or by a free kick, which can score a field goal if the ball goes through the uprights. All free-kick restrictions are in force during this kick.

Can a receiver be blocked or knocked down while he is waiting to catch a kickoff?

The receiver of any kick beyond the line of scrimmage or free-kick line must be given an unmolested opportunity to catch the ball. He definitely cannot be blocked or knocked down while waiting for the ball.

Does a kickoff have to be kicked from the middle of the field on the forty-yard line?

The kicking team may ask the officials to place the ball anywhere between the hashmarks on a kickoff.

Where would a kickoff originate under ordinary circumstances?

The rules of both collegiate and pro football state that the free-kick line or the spot of the kick for the kicking team will be their forty-yard line. On kickoffs after a safety the free-kick line for the kicking team will be their twenty-yard line.

On a kickoff the kicking team requests that the ball be placed on their own thirty-five-yard line instead of the forty-yard line. No penalty has been enforced. Their reason is poor field conditions at the forty. Is this legal?

The kicking team may kick the ball from any spot behind their free-kick line providing it is between the hashmarks. The receiving team must still be ten yards from the original kickers' free-kick line. This is the same in both college and pro ball.

If the kickers elect to kick from their thirty-five-yard line and an offside penalty is called on them, from where is the penalty enforced?

The penalty is enforced from the thirty-five-yard line in both college and pro ball. The ball would then be rekicked from the kicking team's thirty-yard line, and the receiving team's restraining line would be the opponent's forty-yard line.

On the opening kickoff, with everyone ready, the holder of the kick stands and punts the ball downfield. The receiving team returns for a touchdown. Is this legal?

It is a legal return and a touchdown. It is an illegal kick, but the penalty would surely be declined and the touchdown would count. If the penalty were accepted the down would be replayed.

Does the team that scores a touchdown or a field goal always kick off after the score?

This is the way it is usually done, but the rule states that the team scored upon has a choice of kicking or receiving. Once in a while a strong wind has some affect on the choice.

A kickoff hits the flag or pylon at the intersection of the sideline and the goal line. What is the status of the ball?

It is out of bounds in the end zone. A touchback. The corner flags or pylons are always out of bounds in the end zone.

Why are the holder and kicker on kickoffs allowed to be beyond the kicker's restraining line when the ball is kicked?

This exception to the offside rule protects the soccer-style kicker. The mechanics of this kick make it impossible to stay behind the

35 YARDS

40 YARDS

KICKOFF

kicker's line. The holder is allowed this luxury because he gains no advantage by being offside.

Is it necessary for the kicker to be wearing shoes when he kicks?

Shoes are not mandatory equipment in either pro or college ball. Most kickers wear shoes, but once in a while you see one who boots 'em barefooted.

How are the kickers and receivers determined at the start of the second half?

The team that loses the toss of the coin prior to the start of the game has the choice of kicking, receiving, or defending a goal at the start of the second half.

What players are eligible to return a kickoff?

All receiving team players who are inbounds at the time of the kick are eligible to return a kickoff.

If the kickoff goes out of bounds untouched by the receiving team, isn't it true that the receiving team may take the ball at the inbounds spot?

Under college rules the receiving team always has the privilege of taking the ball at the inbounds spot. Pro ball carries no such option. The ball must be rekicked after a five-yard penalty.

A kickoff is bounding inbounds near a sideline where a man on the receiving team, who is standing out of bounds, reaches in and catches the ball. Where will the ball next be put in play?

Under pro rules the ball will be rekicked after a five-yard penalty has been assessed. In college ball, the receiving team must put the ball in play at the inbounds line, since the college code does not consider this a foul for an out-of-bounds kickoff.

A kickoff in flight lands in the end zone, after which it rebounds back onto the field of play, when a member of the receiving team gains possession and runs for a touchdown. Would the touchdown count?

In pro ball it would be scored a touchdown, but in college ball it would result in a touchback. By college ball rule, an untouched kickoff striking the ground in the end zone results in an automatic touchback.

A kickoff in flight lands in the end zone, after which it rebounds onto the field of play, where a member of the kicking team gains possession and the ball is declared dead at that spot. What team next puts the ball in play and where?

In college ball the ruling would be a touchback and the receiving team would put the ball in play on their twenty-yard line. In pro ball, the kicking team would retain possession and the ball would be put in play by them at the point of recovery.

On a kickoff while the ball is in flight (you won't believe this) **it deflates** (the air escapes). **What would an official do?**

The referee would obtain another ball and the ball would be re-kicked without penalty. (I hope I never see it!)

A member of the receiving team catches the ball, and while advancing toward the kicking team's goal line, the ball deflates. Would the deflation of the football have an effect on the result of the play?

In this case the deflated ball would have no effect on the play. Play would resume at the spot of the dead ball after obtaining another ball.

On a kickoff a member of the kicking team goes out of bounds while running downfield. He returns inbounds and recovers the untouched ball after it has traveled the required ten yards. Is this a legal recovery?

No! College and pro rules both prohibit this from happening. Under college rules an out-of-bounds member of the kicking team is prohibited from touching or recovering a kickoff until it is touched by a member of the receiving team on the field of play. Pro rules prohibit any touching or recovering of the ball before it is actually possessed by the receiving team.

Do the college rules specify required positions that must be taken by the receiving team on a kickoff?

The receiving team must be inbounds and is required to have at least five players between ten and fifteen yards of the kicker's free-kick line. Pro ball has no requirements other than they be inbounds and no closer than ten yards from the kicker's free-kick line when the ball is kicked.

Can a backward pass be made on a kickoff?

A backward pass can be made by either team on a kickoff or at any other time during a football game.

If an incompleted backward pass is thrown by the receiving team on a kickoff return and the kicking team picks up the ball, can they advance for a score?

In pro ball as well as college ball the defensive team may only recover a muffed or an incompleted backward pass. The kicking team in the play above becomes the defense, and they cannot advance the ball.

Can a ball be handed forward on a reverse during a kickoff return?

It is a foul whenever a ball is handed forward anywhere but behind the line of scrimmage by the team that originally put the ball in play. Illegal handing carries a five-yard penalty from the spot of the foul. However, the answer to the question is yes, the ball can be handed forward on a kickoff return, but it is a foul. The foul can always be declined if the result of the play benefits the opposing team.

KICKS FROM THE LINE OF SCRIMMAGE

Ohio State was leading 14–11 when exuberant Ohio State fans rushed out onto the field and ripped down the goal posts before the game had ended. What if Michigan had decided they wanted to kick a field goal in the closing seconds?

If that had actually happened, one of the most bizarre plays in the history of college football would have occurred.

Let's set the scene. Both goal posts are down on either end of the field, and the Michigan captain informs the referee of his intended field goal attempt. The referee would have taken time out to confer with the home team management in hopes that spare goal posts were available. Let's say there were none.

Believe it or not, this situation is actually covered in the collegiate rules. Here is the ruling:

Two men would be selected by the referee and placed on the end line at the exact spot where the goal posts stood. They would be twenty-three feet four inches apart, and each man would be sixty-eight feet three inches from the sideline.

Each man would raise his outside arm and the officials would take their places, with the back judge and field judge each standing behind the "human posts."

The ball would be put into play and the judgment on whether or not the kick was good would rest with the officials. They would have to determine whether or not the ball would have made it through the uprights and over the crossbar.

Fortunately, Michigan didn't try for a field goal, and Ohio State won 14–11.

What is a goal post?

"Goal post" is a term used to describe two upright posts with a crossbar used on the end line in college ball and on the goal line in pro ball.

What is an upright?

An upright is one of two standards that support the crossbar of the goal post. The top of the upright must be a minimum of twenty feet above the ground in both pro and college ball.

Are the goal posts the same size in both college and pro ball?

In college ball the goal posts are twenty-three feet four inches wide; the pro goal posts are eighteen feet six inches wide.

Why are the college goal posts on the end line and the pro posts on the goal line?

The rule books do not answer the question, but an educated guess would be as follows: College posts are on the end line because of safety. They are out of the way and not in the field of play. Pro posts are on the goal line to make it easier to kick field goals.

A kick from scrimmage or a kickoff touches the receivers' goal post or crossbar. The kick is not a field goal attempt. Is the ball in play after hitting the post?

The ball is dead the instant it hits the goal post. This rule is the same in college and pro football. The result of the play is a touchback.

A scrimmage kick from the kicker's end zone hits the goal post as it travels out into the field of play. Is it still in play or is it dead?

This touching is ignored, and the ball continues in play. This could only happen in pro ball because the college goal posts would be behind the kicker.

Aren't a muff and a fumble the same thing?

The only similarity between a muff and a fumble is that both are touched by a player. A fumble is when a player who has possession loses the ball other than by passing or kicking. A muff is an unsuccessful attempt to gain possession of the ball, which is touched in the attempt.

A kicked ball becomes a free ball that either team can recover and keep once it is muffed or fumbled. A fumbled ball can be advanced by either team in pro ball. College rules allow an advance by the kicking team if the fumble is recovered in flight only. However, when the kick is muffed, no kicking team man can advance the ball in pro or college football.

What is a kicker?

A kicker is any player who punts, drop kicks, or place kicks the ball according to the rules of the game. He remains the kicker until he has had a reasonable opportunity to regain his balance. He then loses his immunity and can be blocked or tackled.

Can any player on the offensive team be a kicker?

In college ball, any offensive player can line up in the position of the kicker and can legally kick the ball. In pro ball, all players must be numbered by position, and if a player other than one numbered for the backfield wishes to be the kicker, he must report his position change to the referee.

A punter's knee is touching the ground when he fields a low snap from the center. He stands and punts the ball downfield. Is this ball in play?

In college ball the instant the ball is possessed by the punter with his knee on the ground it becomes dead. It is the same as a runner hitting the ground. In pro ball the kick is in play and perfectly legal. The pros can get up and run after they make contact with the ground providing they have not been knocked down by an opponent.

What is considered a scrimmage kick?

A scrimmage kick is a punt, drop kick, or place kick made by the offensive team during a scrimmage down before team possession has changed (not a try for point). The only difference under the rules between a punt and a place kick is that a place kick will score three points or one point if it goes over and through the goal posts, and a punt traveling the same route will score no points.

When a kick is muffed, what actually happens?

A muff is when a player touches the ball in an unsuccessful attempt to obtain possession of it. A muff is not a fumble!

A punt or field goal attempt goes across the line of scrimmage, and before it can be touched by either team it rebounds back behind the line of scrimmage, where a member of the kicking team picks it up and runs. Will a first down be awarded to the kicking team if the runner gains the necessary yardage?

In pro ball it will be a first down for the kickers. Pro rules allow the kickers to advance any kick that rebounds back behind the line of scrimmage except on a try-for-point kick. In college ball it would not be a first down for the kickers. The ball would be dead the instant it was recovered by the kicking team.

A punt or field goal attempt goes across the line of scrimmage and is touched by the receiving team. It then bounces back behind the line of scrimmage, where it is advanced by a member of the kicking team. Will a first down be awarded to the kicking team if the runner gains the necessary yardage?

In both pro and college ball it will be a first down for the kickers. Pro rules allow the kicking team to advance, but even if they do not make the necessary yardage, it will be a first down for them.

College rules do not permit any advance by the kicking team, but it would be an automatic first down for them.

NOTE: Once a scrimmage kick (punt or field goal attempt) is touched by the receiving team beyond the line of scrimmage, it will always be a first down for the recovering team, providing no foul occurs during the play. This is true under both college and pro rules.

A punt or field goal attempt is touched beyond the line of scrimmage and recovered by a member of the kicking team beyond the line of scrimmage. Can the kickers advance?

Pro and college rules both prohibit any advance of this ball. It is a first down for the kicking team at the spot where they gained possession of the ball. The key word is "touched." As long as the kick is not possessed by the receiving team, it may be recovered or caught by members of the kicking team but not advanced.

NOTE: The kicking team may *never* advance their own kick. This is true under both college and pro rules.

What do you mean when you say that a team can't advance their own kick?

A kick remains a kick under pro and college rules until it becomes the possession of the receiving team. It would then become a running play if the receivers advanced the ball.

The kicker is about to punt the ball, but for some reason his foot misses it. The ball hits the ground, and the kicker then kicks the ball downfield directly from the ground. Is this legal?

In both pro and college ball this is illegally kicking the ball. The penalty in college ball is loss of the ball at the spot of the foul. In pro ball the penalty is fifteen yards from the spot of the foul.

A ball is free from a fumble and a player of either team attempts to kick the ball from the ground, but his foot misses the ball. Is this a foul?

In college ball the act is ignored. In order to foul in this situation, the ball would have to be kicked. In pro ball it is a foul just as severe as actually kicking the ball, fifteen yards from the spot of the foul. It is called illegally kicking with the foot.

What is a return kick?

A return kick is a kick by either team after there has been a change of team possession during a down. It is legal in pro ball and illegal in college ball.

What would be considered a change of team possession during a down?

A change of team possession during a down would include a forward or backward pass interception, a fumble recovery, receiving a punt, receiving a field goal attempt, or receiving a kick-off.

Can any member of the team that puts the ball in play kick it from any place on the field, whether he is behind or beyond the line of scrimmage?

Both college and pro rules allow the team that puts the ball in play to punt, drop kick, or place kick from any place behind or beyond the line of scrimmage.

Can any member of the team that has gained possession during a down, by intercepting a pass or fumble or by receiving a kicked ball, kick the ball after gaining possession?

In college ball it is illegal to kick the ball after possession has changed during a down. It is called a return kick and carries a five-yard penalty. In pro ball it is legal to return kick any number of times after possession has changed during a down.

If a punt receiver catches the ball in the playing field and quickly kicks the ball back upfield, who can legally recover and keep the ball?

In college ball it is an illegal kick and the ball is dead the instant it is kicked. The team that return kicked is penalized five yards from the spot of the kick, and it is their ball. In pro ball it is a legal play. Only the team receiving the return kick can recover and keep the ball, unless it is touched by the receivers first and then recovered by the kickers.

What is running into the kicker?

Running into the kicker is covered in pro rules only. It is when an opponent runs into but does not rough the kicker. The penalty is five yards from the line of scrimmage and an automatic first down.

Can you have roughing the kicker on a return kick?

You can't have roughing the kicker on a return kick because it is not reasonably obvious that a kick will be made. A return kick is only legal in pro ball.

What is roughing the kicker, and what is the penalty?

When it is reasonably obvious that the kicker will kick the football, no opponent may block or tackle him until he has had a reasonable opportunity to regain his balance after he kicks the ball. However, if the on-charging opponent touches the ball before he roughs the kicker or if the contact is caused by the kicker's motion, no penalty is called.

In pro ball the penalty is fifteen yards from the line of scrimmage and an automatic first down for the kicking team. In college ball the penalty is fifteen yards from the line of scrimmage, but it is not an automatic first down.

Isn't roughing the kicker always called if the kicker is hit and knocked down by a defensive man who fails to get a piece of the football?

If for some reason it is not obvious that the kick will be made, such as a bad snap from center, an attempted move in any direction by the kicker or a fake pass, the defense is given additional opportunity to get to the kicker.

The snap from center is low and the ball bounces in front of the kicker, who cleanly fields the ball and punts. He is knocked down by a member of the defensive team. Is roughing the kicker called?

This is roughing the kicker. The low snap was cleanly fielded, and it was obvious that the kick was going to be made when the kicker immediately booted the ball. A bad snap doesn't give the defense license to nail the kicker.

A defensive rusher gets a piece of a punted ball as it leaves the kicker's foot. The kicker is then knocked down by another on-charging defensive player a moment later. Is this roughing the kicker?

If the kicker had been hit by the player who got a piece of the kick, it would not be roughing. If anyone other than the player who blocks or partially blocks the kick hits the kicker, it would be roughing the kicker.

A kick is blocked behind the line of scrimmage. The kicker picks up the blocked kick, runs a few steps, and kicks the ball again. He is knocked down by a defensive rusher just as he gets the second kick away. Is this considered roughing the kicker?

This is not roughing the kicker. Kicking the ball twice on a single play is perfectly legal, but once the kicker begins to run after the first kick, it is no longer obvious that he is going to kick the ball again. The defensive team must be allowed to block or tackle the ball carrier, and that is exactly what the kicker becomes when he starts to run.

Is a place kicker given the same protection as a punter?

In both college and pro ball the term "kicker" covers any player who kicks the ball, whether it is a punt, drop kick, or place kick. When a place kick is made, the holder of the place kick is protected just the same as the kicker.

Is roughing the holder of a place kick as severe a penalty as roughing the kicker?

The penalty is exactly the same. The holder of a place kick is just as unprotected while he is holding as the kicker is while he is in the act of kicking. They must both be protected from injury.

Can a member of the kicking team catch their own kick in order to keep it from going into the receiving team's end zone?

In college ball the catch would be legal providing no man on the receiving team is in position to make a catch. So, you see, a team may catch its own kick, but it would still belong to the receiving team at the spot where the kickers caught the ball. Pro rules are the same in this case, with one exception. If the catch is on or inside the receivers' five-yard line and the catcher's momentum carries him into the end zone, the receivers would get the ball on their own twenty-yard line instead of at the spot of the catch.

A kick from scrimmage accidentally hits a member of the kicking team in the back as he is running down under the kick. Is this considered interference with a kicked ball?

It is not a foul for interference unless a man on the receiving team could have caught the kick. It is an illegal touching of the ball by the kicking team, and the receiving team can have the ball put in play at the spot of illegal touching after the play is over.

A member of the kicking team, who is downfield, falls on the untouched ball at the receiving team's ten-yard line. Is this a legal play?

This is called downing the ball. It is a good play by the kicking team and is perfectly legal. It keeps the ball from going into the end zone for a touchback. The receivers have to put the ball in play at the ten-yard line instead of the twenty because of the downing. The ball still belongs to the receiving team whenever an untouched kick is downed beyond the line by a member of the kicking team.

A member of the kicking team tries to down an untouched scrimmage kick on or inside the receiving team's five-yard line, but when he dives onto the ball his momentum carries him and the ball into the receiving team's end zone. Where is the ball put into play?

In college ball the play would have been blown dead at the spot where the kicking team man gained possession of the ball. If he had grabbed the ball on the three and had rolled into the end zone, the receiving team would be given the ball on the three-yard line.

In pro ball the rule is different in this situation. The play would result in a touchback. Any kick that is downed on or inside the receivers' five-yard line with the kicking team man's momentum carrying him into the end zone is considered a touchback.

A member of the kicking team tries to down an untouched scrimmage kick anywhere outside of the receivers' five-yard line, and his momentum carries him into the end zone. Where is the ball put into play?

In college and pro ball the ball will be put into play at the spot where the kicking team player gained possession. If he grabbed it at the six-yard line and rolled into the end zone it would be put into play at the six-yard line.

What is forced touching of the football?

Forced touching is when a man is blocked or pushed into contact with the ball by an opponent. In college ball, unless the man who is blocked or pushed into the ball touches it with a hand or hands, the touching is ignored. In pro ball any forced touching is ignored even if the ball touches the hands. When touching is ignored it is as if it did not happen.

A punt or field goal attempt is rolling near the receivers' one-yard line when a kicking team man blocks a receiver into the football and the ball bounces into the receivers' end zone. The kicking team man then falls on the ball. Isn't this a touchdown for the kicking team?

In college ball if the receiver, who was blocked into the ball, touches the ball with his hand, it would be a touchdown for the kicking team. In pro ball it would be a touchback and the receiving team would get the ball on their own twenty-yard line, first and ten. The touching would be ignored.

Fourth down and fifteen yards to go for Bowling Green University. Purdue blocks their punt, and the ball goes straight up into the air. It bounces behind the line of scrimmage, and the man who kicked it picks it up and runs twenty yards before he is downed. First down for Bowling Green. Why did the defensive team allow the kicker to run with the recovered kick?

Why the defense allowed the kicker to run is only a guess on my part. I can tell you that punts or field goal attempts cause more problems for players than almost any other play in football. Players get confused, and so do the fans. In pro and college ball the rule concerning blocked kicks is exactly the same. If a kick fails to cross the line of scrimmage, anyone can recover and advance the ball. Sounds simple, but in the heat of battle it's just plain confusing.

What is a blocked kick?

A blocked kick is a kick that is touched or blocked by a player, keeping the ball from crossing the line of scrimmage. The blocked kick can be caught and advanced by either team behind the line of scrimmage.

Who can block a kick?

It is usually a defensive rusher who blocks the kick, but once in a while a kicking team man who is blocking for the kicker is pushed back into the ball or he steps back and the ball hits him. Anyone can block a kick.

A blocked punt is rolling behind the line of scrimmage when a player of either team, in an attempt to pick up the ball, forces the ball across the line of scrimmage. Can the ball be recovered and kept by either team?

Any touching of the ball behind the line of scrimmage is ignored by rule once the ball crosses the line of scrimmage. If the kickers recover beyond the line of scrimmage the ball would be awarded to the receiving team. Pro and college rules are the same in this situation.

A punt is blocked and the kicker catches the rebounding ball, drops back a few yards, and throws a forward pass. Is this legal?

It is perfectly legal in both pro and college ball. However, it is more than likely that ineligible receivers will be downfield.

A team punts on third down and the kick is blocked behind the line of scrimmage. The kicking team recovers the ball behind the line. Who gets the ball, and what down would it be?

The ball would still belong to the kicking team, and it would be fourth down. The touching behind the line is ignored and the play is treated like a run or pass play. The offense would have one more down.

Who can run with a blocked kick that does not cross the scrimmage line?

A blocked kick or one that is not blocked that does not cross the scrimmage line can be caught, recovered, or advanced by either the kickers or the receivers.

NOTE: Any scrimmage kick that fails to cross the line of scrimmage is treated by rule as a regular running play. This is true in both college and pro football.

A kick is blocked behind the line of scrimmage and the kicker picks up the ball, runs to his left, and then kicks it again. Is the second kick legal?

The kick is perfectly legal. Both college and pro rules allow the team that put the ball in play to kick from any place on the field. The blocked kick is not considered a kick by rule.

It is second down and a punt goes out of bounds behind the line of scrimmage. Who will put the ball in play on the next down?

Any punt that goes out of bounds behind the line of scrimmage belongs to the receiving team at the spot that it went out, regardless of the down.

A punt comes down behind the line of scrimmage, and for some reason no one makes an attempt to recover the ball. The official finally blows the ball dead. Who gets the ball?

Regardless of the down, the ball will be awarded to the receiving team. If it had been second down, the kickers could have recovered the ball and it would have been third down.

A kick from scrimmage is blown dead beyond the line of scrimmage with no team in possession. In other words, no one wants the ball. Who gets it?

The ball is awarded to the receiving team. A kicked ball that is blown dead in no player's possession is awarded by rule to the receiving team.

A kick from scrimmage is recovered by two opposing players at the same time. Who gets the ball?

After the simultaneous recovery of a kick, the ball is awarded to the receiving team. Whenever a kicked ball is recovered by two opponents at the same time it is awarded to the receivers.

What is a fair catch?

It is an unhindered catch by any member of the receiving team of any kick that has crossed the kicking team's line of scrimmage or free-kick line, providing a proper signal has been given by the receiver.

What is the legal signal for a fair catch?

The pro rules require one hand raised at full arm's length above the head. The college rules require one hand and arm extended above the head and moving them from side to side.

Can the ball be advanced after a fair catch is made?

The pro rules prohibit any advance of the ball once a fair catch signal is made and the ball is caught by any member of the receiving team. If the ball hits the ground, any one on the receiving team may advance the ball. The man who signals for the fair catch is protected from being tackled or blocked until the ball has hit the ground. Even if he muffs the ball, he remains protected until the ball has hit the ground.

Collegiate rules prohibit any advance once a fair-catch signal is given, even if the ball is not caught. Once the ball hits the ground, only the receiving team may recover. The man who signals for the fair catch is only protected on his first attempt to catch the ball. If he muffs it he may be hit by members of the kicking team.

A player on the receiving team is standing with a foot out of bounds when he gives a fair-catch signal. Is this a legal signal?

It is a legal signal in both college and pro ball. The defensive team (the receiving team in this case) is not restricted to being inbounds during the play. However, in order to make a good catch he would have to be completely inbounds. In college ball the defense can be out of bounds at the snap or on a kickoff. In pro ball all players must be inbounds at the time of the snap or kickoff.

A fair-catch signal is given but the ball falls short and the man who signaled picks up the ball and runs. Is this legal?

In pro ball the advance is legal. In college ball the advance is illegal and incurs a five-yard penalty for delay of game. The ball would belong to the receivers after the penalty was enforced.

A fair-catch signal is given but the signaler misjudges the ball and it hits his shoulder and bounces into the air. Another member of the receiving team catches the ball in flight and advances. Is this a legal advance?

In both pro and college ball, if a receiver gives a fair-catch signal during a kick that crosses the line of scrimmage, the ball is dead when it is caught by any member of the receiving team, even if they did not give the signal.

A fair-catch signal is given, but the signaler muffs the ball and it hits a member of the kicking team and is then caught or recovered by a player on the receiving team. Can he run with the ball?

In pro ball any receiver can advance the ball once the kickers touch it. In college ball the receivers can only recover.

What is fair-catch interference or kick-catch interference?

Fair-catch or kick-catch interference is as follows: During any kick that crosses the line of scrimmage, no player on the kicking team will interfere with any receiver who can reach the kick in flight. He will also not interfere with the ball in flight or block the path of the receiver to the ball.

What is the penalty for fair-catch or kick-catch interference?

In pro and college ball it is a fifteen-yard penalty from the spot of the foul, and the fair catch is also awarded to the receiving team.

The intended receiver of a punt is running to make the catch when a member of the kicking team blocks his path to the ball. The intended receiver runs around the man and makes the catch. Is this a legal play?

It is an interference foul even though no contact resulted. The receiver had to run out of his direct path. In both college and pro ball it is a foul.

Explain the free kick rule in pro ball in regard to a fair catch.

The rule is only used in pro ball. The team making a fair catch may choose to put the ball in play with either a regular scrimmage play or a free kick. The free kick may score a field goal. The defense may be no closer than ten yards from the ball when it is kicked. The ball is also free and may be recovered by either team if a field goal is not scored. If a free kick is to be tried it must be done without the use of a "tee."

After a fair catch is made, the receiving team elects to free kick. The ball lands in the end zone and bounces out to the one-yard line. The kicking team recovers on the one-yard line and runs into the end zone for a touchdown. Is this a legal advance?

A free kick that travels ten yards is a free ball and the recovery on the one-yard line is legal. The advance is not legal. The ball can only be recovered, but it is a first down and goal to go for the kicking team at their opponents' one-yard line. This play is only possible under the pro rules. College rules do not permit a free kick after a fair catch.

If a punt or place kick goes into the end zone is it a dead ball or does the receiving team have the option to run the ball out?

In college ball it is an automatic touchback if a kicked ball lands in the receivers' end zone before being touched by a member of the receiving team. If the receivers touch the ball before it lands in the end zone, they have the option of recovering or running the ball. In pro ball it is not an automatic touchback if the ball lands in the end zone. The receivers may choose to run any kicked ball out of their own end zone.

A player on the receiving team catches a punt or an attempted field goal in the field of play and his momentum carries him into his own end zone, where he is downed. Where is the ball next put in play?

In both pro and college ball this play would result in a safety. Score two points for the kicking team. The force that put the ball into the end zone came from the man who made the catch.

A punt lands in the receivers' end zone and bounces back into the field of play and rolls out of bounds on the two-yard line. Where is the ball put in play?

In college ball it is an automatic touchback by rule. In pro ball it is the receiving team's ball first and ten at their two-yard line.

The punter is back in his end zone waiting for the ball to be snapped. His foot is touching the end line of the end zone. He is still touching the line when he receives the ball from the center. Is this a foul?

The instant the punter receives the ball from the center while he is touching the end line, the play is over and the ball is dead. The man on the end line is out of bounds, and when the ball touches him it is also out of bounds. This play would result in a safety. Score two points for the receiving team.

The punter is back in his end zone waiting for the ball to be snapped. He is standing on the end line as the ball is snapped but moves into the end zone as he catches the snap and he punts. Is this legal?

In both pro and college ball the offensive team must be in bounds when the ball is snapped. The kick is legal but the offense has fouled and is assessed five yards from the previous line of scrimmage for illegal formation if the penalty is accepted.

Does a team have to punt on fourth down?

A team doesn't ever have to punt the ball, but when they have not made a first down and are in their own territory, it is the thing to do.

Can a team punt on first, second, or third down?

A team can punt on any down from any spot on the field.

A punt or attempted field goal hits an official in the field of play. Does the ball become dead?

An official is considered part of the playing field. The ball continues in play just as if it hadn't touched the official.

The Cleveland Browns were ahead by several touchdowns with only a short time remaining in the game. They had the ball on or about their opponents' ten-yard line. The back-up quarterback was sent into the game, and everyone in the stands felt certain that the Browns would score again before the final gun. The new quarterback called his play and, to the surprise of all, he punted the ball clean out of the stadium. Yes, he punted from his opponents' ten-yard line. Did someone ask if you could punt from anywhere on the field?

BASIC SCRIMMAGE REQUIREMENTS AND RUNNING PLAYS

Whether you are sitting in the stands or in front of a television screen, most fans assume that teams merely take positions on opposite sides of the field when playing a game of football. On every play we recognize the sight of opposing linemen in relatively the same positions. The same is true for the backs. We see varied offensive and defensive formations common to today's game. To the average fan it appears to be a simple thing for a team to line up and run a play. Far from true! A team, whether on offense or defense, is required to incorporate not only the technical fundamentals of the game, but also to recognize the rule requirements to which they must adhere, to legally put the ball in play. It looks and sounds simple, but once you've read this chapter you will agree that a player is required to be alert and to think at all times during a game. He must be ready mentally as well as physically. Yes, football rules are complicated.

One of the greatest runs I have ever seen came early in the third quarter of an Ohio State vs. Iowa game played at Ohio State in the mid-1960s. The game was close and both teams were moving between the thirty-five-yard lines with little scoring success.

I had just spotted the ball and was waiting for the offensive team to break out of the huddle when the near "sleeping" crowd started to yell. I looked around quickly to see what had caused this reaction, and then I saw the "star" of the day just emerging from under the temporary stands at the open end of Ohio Stadium. It was a pretty solid, very frightened cottontail rabbit, and he ran the entire hundred yards in about five seconds flat to a thundering roar from the throng of eighty-five thousand fans. He circled in the end zone and down the other sideline he came, to the great delight of the crowd.

He crossed the goal line for his second touchdown and disappeared under the stand whence he came. The crowd was on its feet cheering like no crowd had ever cheered. The game continued after the slight delay and ended with Ohio State winning by a few points. It really wasn't the most exciting football game played that year, but the fans, the players, and the officials will never forget the rabbit that ran for two touchdowns without ever having a hand touch him.

What is meant by first and ten?

First and ten is when a new series of four downs is awarded to a team. They have to gain ten or more yards in the next four downs in order to keep possession of the ball.

When is a team awarded a first and ten?

When they have gained the necessary yardage during the last series, when a penalty leaves the ball beyond the line to gain, after a touchback, after a possession change, and after the kicking team recovers their own kick after it has been touched by a receiving team man beyond the line of scrimmage.

What is the "line to gain"?

The line to gain is the yard line on the field that the offensive team must reach with the ball in order to be awarded another new series and a first down.

When a ball carrier's knees hit the ground, what determines where the ball is next put into play: the spot where his knees hit the ground or the spot where the ball is when the knees hit the ground?

The position of the ball when the knees hit the ground determines the forward progress point and the spot where the ball will next be snapped.

May a coach request a measurement?

In both college and pro ball the captain or his designated representative must request a measurement. The coach is not granted this privilege.

Who is responsible for determining the forward progress of a runner?

The primary responsibility of determining forward progress belongs to the head linesman or line judge (the field judge in five-man crews). However, depending upon the position of the ball, any one of the crew of officials can indicate forward progress.

LINE OF FORWARD PROGRESS

When marking the spot, the head linesman and the line judge do so in an inconspicuous way, noticeable only to those in the "know." Next time you are at a game, see if you can detect which official is holding the progress point.

Why does the quarterback call out certain numbers before the ball is snapped?

The offensive team is told by the quarterback in the huddle when the ball is to be snapped. The signal to snap is usually a verbal one given by the quarterback. He usually calls out numbers, but some quarterbacks use colors or just sounds. When the specified number, color, sound, etc., is heard, the ball is snapped and the play begins.

Why does the quarterback yell his signals so loudly?

He wants his teammates to hear him above the crowd noise. Today's crowds are very large and very noisy, and it is very important that the signals are heard by the offensive team, enabling them to move together on the signal.

Can a team break the huddle and immediately put the ball into play without delay, once they get to the ball?

Once the offense breaks from the huddle, the entire team must be stationary at the same time for a full second before the snap. The penalty for an illegal shift is five yards.

Wouldn't it save a lot of time if a team didn't use a huddle, or is a huddle required by rule?

It is not necessary to have a huddle before each play, and a team can go directly to the line of scrimmage as soon as the preceding play is blown dead. Omitting a huddle would definitely save time and many more plays could be run. This is usually done when time is running out.

How is the play called if there is no huddle?

The quarterback calls an automatic or an audible play at the line, which is identified by means of a verbal signal.

What is meant by defensive signal jamming?

Signal jamming is when a defensive player or players makes an attempt to confuse the offensive team by calling out similar sounds or numbers, etc., at the same time that the quarterback is calling out his signals. This is designed to cause the offensive team to move too soon. It is an unsportsmanlike act and carries a fifteen-yard penalty in both college and pro ball.

Are linemen and backs required to wear certain numbers on their jerseys?

In collegiate ball the rules strongly recommend that offensive players be numbered accordingly:

Centers	50 to 59
Guards	60 to 69
Tackles	70 to 79
Ends	80 to 89
Backs	1 to 49

All players must be numbered 1 to 99, with at least five offensive players on the line of scrimmage numbered 50 to 79.

In pro ball offensive and defensive players are numbered by positions:

Quarterbacks and kickers	1 to 19
All running and defensive backs	20 to 49
Centers and linebackers	50 to 59
Offensive guards, tackles, and defensive linemen	60 to 79
Wide receivers and tight ends	80 to 89

Numbers in the 90s will be permitted only in preseason games when team rosters are large. All players who were in the league during the 1972 season may use their old numbers if they wish.

If the home team and the visiting team have similarly colored jerseys, who has to change?

In both college and pro ball the visiting team has to make the jersey change.

Must all players on a team wear helmets of the same color?

In college ball all players on any given team must wear helmets of the same color. In pro ball it is optional for eligible pass receivers to wear a different color helmet than their teammates, but if any one receiver wears a helmet of a different color, all receivers on that team must wear the same color.

Are all players required to wear face masks?

Players in pro and college ball have found it necessary to have face masks attached to their helmets. The pro rule stipulates that the face mask not be more than five-eighths inch in diameter, be of a rounded material, and be made of Lucite, clear plastic, or a similar material. The college rule calls for the face mask to be made of nonbreakable molded plastic with rounded edges or of a rounded metal material, having all surfaces covered with rubber or a similar resilient material.

May a player grab an opponent's face mask?

It is illegal to grab an opponent's face mask in both pro and college ball. The collegiate penalty is fifteen yards from the spot of the foul. The pro rule dictates a five-yard penalty for merely grabbing the face mask and a fifteen-yard penalty for flagrantly grabbing the mask.

Are players required by rule to wear a mouth protector?

Pro football does not require its players to wear mouth protectors. College football rules require all players to use a properly fitted mouth protector. It sure saves the teeth!

May offensive players be standing in an erect position on the line of scrimmage or in the backfield when the ball is snapped?

Offensive linemen and backs can be in an erect position as long as they are not moving at the snap, with the exception of one man, who can legally be in motion at the snap. Offensive linemen are usually in a three-point stance, but if they wish to stand erect it is perfectly legal.

What is a three- or a four-point stance?

When a player is in a crouched position with one hand on the ground and his back almost parallel to the ground he is in a three-point stance. If both hands are on the ground it is a four-point stance.

What are the requirements for a player on offense to be considered a backfield man?

A backfield man must take a position at least one yard behind the line of scrimmage. An exception to this is the quarterback, who is permitted to take a position enabling him to receive a hand-to-hand snap from the center.

Can offensive linemen line up facing the center instead of facing their opponents?

In both college and pro ball, all offensive linemen must have their shoulders parallel to the line of scrimmage and facing their opponents' goal line.

Can the offensive team have more than seven men on the line of scrimmage?

The offensive team can have as many as eleven men on the line of scrimmage. The rules require that the offensive team have at least seven men on the line, but no backs are required by rule. It would be very difficult to operate without backs, but it would be legal.

Is the defensive team required to have a certain number of players on the line of scrimmage at the snap?

The defense can have any number of men on the line or no men on the line. The defense has no special requirements on scrimmage plays except that in pro ball all defensive men must be inbounds at the snap. In college ball the defense is not required to be inbounds at the snap.

Is it permissible for a back to switch positions with a lineman during a scrimmage play?

In pro ball any player switching position must report the change to the referee. The penalty for not reporting a change in position with regard to eligibility is fifteen yards. In college ball the players can switch without reporting to an official providing they have at least five players wearing a number between 50 and 79 in the line of scrimmage.

How close to the line of scrimmage must an offensive lineman be at the snap?

An offensive lineman must be within twelve inches of the line of scrimmage when the ball is snapped. As long as some part of his body is within the twelve inches, it is legal. He must be facing his opponents' goal line.

Are offensive linemen required to be any lateral distance from their teammates on the line of scrimmage at the snap?

The only distance requirement for offensive linemen is that they be within twelve inches of the line of scrimmage at the snap and that they be motionless once they have set. Laterally, linemen can be as far apart as they wish.

Can a team ever be permitted to put the ball in play in the side zone?

According to the rule in college and pro ball, all scrimmage plays or free kicks must be made from between the inbounds lines with the exception of a fourth-down punt on or inside a team's own fifteen-yard line in pro ball. In this situation the ball is moved to a special inbounds marker that is twenty yards from the sideline.

What is a shift?

A shift is the movement of two or more offensive players prior to the snap of the ball, who after having been in a set position, simultaneously change their positions.

What is an illegal shift?

This occurs when two or more offensive players are moving when the ball is snapped, or when two or more offensive players who have moved simultaneously fail to set for one full second before the ball is snapped.

What is the difference between an illegal shift and illegal motion?

Illegal motion is when one offensive player is moving toward the line of scrimmage at the snap and an illegal shift is when two or more offensive players are moving or have not stopped for one second when the ball is snapped. Both fouls incur five-yard penalties.

May two men of the same team be in motion at the snap?

Only one man can be legally in motion at the snap for the offensive team. The defense can have all eleven in motion. The defense has no motion restrictions.

After the offensive team has legally set for one full second, a back starts to move toward the line of scrimmage and stops just before the snap. He is not set for a full second. Is this legal?

This is a legal play. Once the entire offense has set for a full second and only one man moves, he may continue moving laterally or away from the line of scrimmage or he may move toward the line and need only be stationary at the snap. He does not have to be set for a full second, as in a shift. The crowd always yells that this is illegal motion and so do the coaches, but it's a legal play and always has been.

Can an offensive back move around before the snap on a kick play?

A foul for one player illegally in motion does not occur until the ball has been snapped. Movement prior to the snap is not illegal.

Can the quarterback go in motion on a scrimmage play?

The quarterback may legally be in motion in both college and pro ball.

May an offensive lineman be in motion at the snap of the ball?

In pro ball it is illegal for a lineman to be in motion at the snap. The only player who can be legally in motion at the snap is the one backfield man who is moving parallel to or backward from the line of scrimmage. In college ball a lineman can legally be in motion at the snap, providing he is five or more yards behind the line of scrimmage at the snap and providing his team complies with the rule of having seven men on the line of scrimmage.

Don't all offensive players have to be set and completely still for one full second prior to the snap of the ball?

After a huddle all offensive players must be set at the same time for one full second. After they have all set, if two or more men move again, the entire offensive team must again be set at the same time for a full second.

How can the offensive team be penalized for illegal procedure or false start long before the ball is snapped?

In both college and pro ball the offensive interior linemen (those linemen who are positioned between the center and the man on the end of the line) are restricted from any movement once they have taken a three- or four-point stance or once they have simulated a stance by putting a hand or hands near the ground. The foul is called as soon as the movement is detected. This illegal procedure or false start on the part of the offense usually occurs prior to the snap of the ball. The penalty is five yards.

Can the defensive team jump in and out of the neutral zone without being penalized?

In both pro and college ball the defensive team can jump into and out of the neutral zone, providing they do not make contact with, or draw a charge from, the offense. If the jumping is repeated in pro ball the man will receive a warning from the official, and if it continues, a five-yard penalty will be assessed.

What constitutes an offside?

A player of either team is offside when any part of his body is beyond the line of scrimmage or his free-kick line when the ball is put into play.

What is clipping?

Clipping is throwing the body across the back of the legs of an opponent or charging or falling into the back of an opponent after approaching him from the rear, unless he is the ball carrier or unless he is in the legal clip zone.

What is the legal clip zone?

Under the pro rules, the area where it is legal to clip is a rectangle extending laterally to the positions usually occupied by defensive tackles and three yards on either side of the line of scrimmage. This zone covers close line play and is no longer considered to exist once the play develops. The legal clip must be made within a few seconds of the snap or it will probably be a foul. The legal clip zone in college ball is a rectangular area centered on the *middle* lineman of the offensive team and extends four yards laterally in each direction and three yards on either side of the line of scrimmage. This zone also disappears as soon as the play develops. In both college and pro ball, once the legal clip zone disintegrates, any clip is a foul.

What is hurdling and what is the penalty for it?

Pro ball has two types of hurdling. Both incur fifteen-yard penalties. Hurdling in the open is when a runner jumps over an opponent who is on his feet. Hurdling in the line is when the runner jumps over a player on the line of scrimmage with both feet or both knees foremost, within five yards on either side of the spot of the snap. College rules define hurdling as an attempt by a runner to jump with one or both feet or knees foremost over a player who is on his feet. The penalty is fifteen yards.

What is the collegiate crack back block rule?

Any offensive player who is positioned more than nine yards from the ball at the snap is prevented from blocking below the waist when moving to the inside toward the spot where the ball was snapped. This prohibited area extends three yards on either side of the line of scrimmage, and from sideline to sideline. The rule is in effect until the ball is advanced beyond the restricted zone.

Can a player who is flanked wide come in and block a linebacker or an end from the blind side on the line of scrimmage?

In pro ball it is legal providing the block is not a clip. In college ball it is an illegal crack back block if the block is below the waist.

Would it be considered illegal if a player hid the ball under his jersey?

No player may hide the ball under his clothing or substitute any other article, such as a helmet, for the ball. The penalty in college and pro ball is fifteen yards.

May you trip a ball carrier?

It is illegal for a player of either team to trip any player on the opposing team, including the ball carrier. The penalty is fifteen yards from the spot of the foul.

May you trip an opponent when attempting to block him?

It is illegal to trip anyone anywhere on the field of play.

When running ahead of the ball carrier, is it legal for offensive players to lock arms while blocking?

This is an illegal act in both pro and college ball. It is called interlocked interference. The penalty in pro ball is fifteen yards from the spot of the foul. In college ball the penalty is five yards from the spot of the foul.

Immediately after the snap, may a defensive lineman slap his opponent on the helmet with an open hand?

In pro ball it is legal to contact an opponent above the shoulders with the open hand if the act occurs during the initial line charge. In college ball it is an illegal act to contact an opponent above the shoulders with a blow from the open hand even on the initial line charge.

Is it legal to tackle a back who is faking possession of the ball?

In pro ball any player who pretends to have the ball may be tackled provided he is crossing or has crossed his line of scrimmage. In college ball the player pretending to have the ball may be tackled behind or beyond the line of scrimmage.

Can offensive linemen lock legs when they take their position at the snap?

Locking legs is illegal for all offensive linemen except those linemen who are adjacent to the center. Only these three linemen can lock legs on any offensive play. Defensive players are not restricted. The rule on locking legs is the same in college and pro ball.

May an offensive lineman use his hands when making a block?

The pro definition of a legal block goes like this: The hands must be cupped or closed and must remain inside the blocker's elbows. The hands must also remain inside the frame of the opponent as well as the blocker's body. The arms may be in a flexed position, but they cannot be fully extended forward to create a push. The college definition states that when an offensive player uses a hand or forearm in blocking or to supplement a shoulder block, the hands must be in contact with the blocker's body and the hands and arms must be kept below the shoulders of their opponents during the block.

May defensive men use their hands to avoid being blocked?

Defensive players are allowed to use their hands in order to avoid being blocked by an opponent.

What is a fumble?

A fumble is a loss of possession of the football by a player other than by passing or kicking it.

Is it a fumble when a runner is tackled and his knees hit the ground first, with his upper body momentarily in an upright position, and immediately thereafter and simultaneous with the knees hitting the ground, he loses possession of the ball?

It is not a fumble. The ball is declared dead the instant the knees make contact with the ground (even though the whistle had not been blown), and the ball will next be put in play from the spot where the ball was positioned when the knees hit the ground.

Is it permissible by rule to push an opponent to get at a fumble or a muffed ball?

Whenever a ball is free from a fumble or a muff, any player can push an opponent in an attempt to recover the ball. However, if one player pushes an opponent so that a teammate can recover the free ball, a penalty for illegal use of the hands will be assessed.

Can either team recover and advance a grounded lateral pass?

In both college and pro ball the defense can only recover a grounded lateral pass. The instant it recovers, the ball becomes dead. The offense can advance the grounded lateral.

Is there any rule against stealing the ball from the ball carrier?

While the ball is in play and in player possession it may legally be stolen by any player on the field.

The offensive ball carrier fumbles the ball near the sideline, and it is last touched by a defensive player before going out of bounds. Who gets the ball for the next play?

A fumbled ball that goes out of bounds belongs to the team last in possession. Touching by the defense has no effect on the ruling. The ball still belongs to the offense.

Can both teams advance a fumbled ball?

In pro ball both the offensive and defensive players can advance a fumbled ball whether it is recovered in flight or picked up from the ground. In college ball only the offense can pick up their fumble from the ground and advance. The defense can only recover a grounded fumble. Both teams can advance a fumble recovered in flight.

A runner fumbles on or about the opponents' five-yard line and the ball bounces into the end zone. Another member of the offensive team recovers the ball in the end zone. Wouldn't this be a touchdown?

In college ball it would be a touchdown. The pro rule is a little different. If the ball is fumbled on or inside the opponents' ten-yard line on fourth down, only the man who fumbled can recover and retain the ball at the spot of recovery. If any other offensive man, other than the fumbling player, recovers, the next play will be snapped from the spot of the fumble. If the fumble occurs on any other down it would be a touchdown.

The runner gains ten yards on a play from scrimmage and then fumbles the ball. The defensive team recovers. Who gets credit for the ten-yard gain?

The runner would be credited with the ten-yard gain. Whether the fumble is recovered by a member of the offense or defense makes no difference statistically.

The ball carrier gains two yards and then fumbles, but the ball is recovered by a teammate five yards farther downfield. Who gets credit for the yardage on the play? What if the fumble had gone out of bounds?

The runner would be credited with a two-yard gain. The additional five yards would be included in total team yardage, but no individual player would get credit for the five yards. If the ball had gone out of bounds instead of being recovered, the credit of yards would be exactly the same.

What is the snap?

The snap is the act of handing or passing the ball back from its position on the ground with a quick continuous motion of the hand or hands.

What is the center?

The center is the offensive lineman who has the job of snapping the ball at the start of all scrimmage plays.

Can the center be offside at the snap?

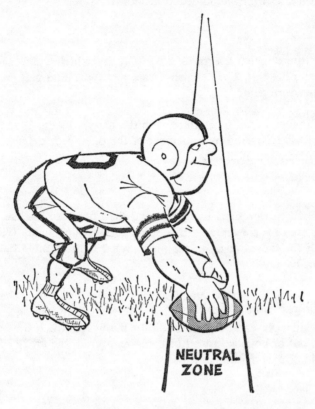

NEUTRAL
ZONE

The center may be offside at the snap providing he is only beyond his own line of scrimmage and not beyond the defensive line of scrimmage. The length of the ball is the distance the center may be beyond his line of scrimmage without incurring a penalty.

If the center lifts the ball from the ground just prior to the snap, can a defensive player grab the ball and keep it?

The snap does not legally start until the ball starts its backward movement. When a center lifts the ball it does not put the ball into play. The defense cannot recover a dead ball. The offense has fouled by lifting the ball, and after the penalty of five yards has been assessed, the ball still belongs to the offensive team.

What is a false snap or an illegal snap?

A false or illegal snap is any act committed by the center that actually simulates the start of the play by pretending to snap the ball before he actually snaps it.

Can the center move his hands to another position on the ball after he has assumed his final position before the snap?

The snapper or center is permitted to adjust the ball once immediately after coming out of the huddle, after which he may not lift a hand or hands from the ball once he has it in his grasp. This is an illegal snap or a false start and carries a five-yard penalty.

Does the ball have to be snapped between the legs of the center?

It is not necessary for the center to snap the ball between his legs, but it is the recommended method.

Is the center required to snap the ball with two hands?

The center may snap the ball with one or two hands. The only requirement is that the movement of the ball during the snap be one quick and continuous motion, with the ball actually leaving or being taken from the snapper's hand or hands.

Can the ball be snapped to any member of the offensive team?

A direct snap of the ball can go only to a player who is legally in the backfield. If the snap hits the ground or an eligible receiver, it can then be picked up by any offensive player.

It is quite obvious to most fans that the center or snapper in both pro and college ball, when snapping for a punt, picks up the ball, moves it forward slightly, and then sends it "zinging" back to the punter. Isn't this an illegal snap?

A legal snap is handing or passing the ball back from its position on the ground with a quick and continuous motion of the hand or hands. Theoretically, the play described is illegal. However, common sense dictates that no foul be called. There is no distinct advantage gained by this action. If the ball is deflected by a defensive player before the snap, the offensive team will be charged with a foul for an illegal snap.

A ball carrier contacts an opponent or an official who is positioned on the sideline. Is the ball carrier out of bounds?

Under the pro rules the ball is out of bounds when, while it is in player possession, it touches a boundary line or anything other than a player on or outside of the boundary line. In the play described, the ball would remain in play if the ball carrier contacted a player out of bounds. If the contact was with an official instead of a player, it would be ruled out of bounds. The college rule is the same as the pro rule except that contact with an official or a player out of bounds would keep the ball in play. Therefore, in either case the ball remains in play.

May a ball carrier use the back of a teammate as a springboard to gain yardage?

This is perfectly legal in pro and college ball.

Do the rules limit the number of ball exchanges during a down?

There are no limitations on the number of legal ball exchanges during a given down.

Can a ball be handed forward beyond the line of scrimmage or after possession has changed during the down?

The ball can never be handed forward beyond the line of scrimmage or after a change of possession. If a forward handing of the ball is attempted and the ball falls to the ground, it becomes a fumble. The penalty for illegal handing of the ball forward is five yards from the spot of the foul.

A ball carrier is on his opponents' two-yard line and going in to score a touchdown. He throws the ball, thinking he has already crossed the goal line. What happens in this case?

It all depends on the direction in which he throws the ball. If it is thrown forward it is an illegal forward pass and the penalty would be five yards from the spot of the pass and loss of the down. If he throws it laterally or backward, the ball would be in play and a member of his team could pick it up and advance. If a backward pass is recovered by a player of the opposing team, it would be their ball at the spot of recovery.

A ball carrier is running down the sideline clearly in the open when he is tackled by a substitute who comes charging from the team area to make the stop. What is the penalty?

In both college and pro ball a touchdown can be awarded if, in the opinions of the officials, the runner would have scored.

Is the ball carrier permitted to use a blow with the forearm in his attempt to get past a defender?

In both college and pro ball this is illegal use of the hand or arm. Any time a player, including the ball carrier, delivers a blow with the forearm, it is a foul.

Can a runner who slips and falls while he is out in the open get up and run again during the same play?

Pro rules allow a ball carrier to get up and advance if a slip caused him to go down. College rules do not allow an advance. Once a college runner is down for any reason, the down ends.

Can a teammate assist a runner by pushing or pulling him forward when he is in the grasp of an opponent?

A player on offense cannot push or pull a teammate in such a way as to assist him in gaining additional yardage. This is called aiding the runner, and in pro ball it is a fifteen-yard penalty. In college ball the penalty for this foul is a five-yard walk-off.

Is it permissible for teammates of the runner or passer to lock arms with one another when blocking on the line of scrimmage?

In both pro and college ball it is an illegal act. It is called interlocked interference, and in pro ball the penalty is fifteen yards from the spot of the foul. In college ball it is a five-yard penalty from the spot of the foul.

PASS PLAYS

The Pittsburgh Steelers were about to lose a very important play-off game to the Oakland Raiders. With only seconds remaining, the Pittsburgh quarterback dropped back to pass, but was forced to scramble and finally unleashed a desperate throw to one of his receivers. As the intended receiver reached up for the ball he was hit by an Oakland defensive back and the ball went flying back in the direction whence it came. A Pittsburgh running back who was looking for someone to block caught the ball in midair and miraculously ran it forty-two yards for the winning touchdown.

The pro rule in this situation is very different from the college rule. In pro ball a legal forward pass may not be touched by two eligible pass receivers on the same play unless the ball is touched by a defending player before it touches the second offensive receiver. The officials ruled that the touchdown was legal because the defensive back, in his attempt to break up the play, had touched the ball. This made the Pittsburgh hero an eligible receiver.

The collegiate rule is much easier to understand and consequently easier to officiate. Any number of eligible receivers may touch the football on a legal forward pass. A defender need not touch the ball for the play to be legal.

Complicated or not, this play will go down as one of the most exciting in the history of football, college or pro.

What is a legal forward pass?

The only legal forward pass in both college and pro ball is the first pass thrown by the offensive team from behind their line of scrimmage and before any possession has changed during the down.

In college and pro ball, how many men may go out for a forward pass and how many men have to stay on the line of scrimmage?

In college ball the eligible receivers, or those men who are permitted to go downfield on a forward pass play, are all offensive players who are legally in the backfield and wearing any number other than 50 through 79, and those men on the end of the line of scrimmage wearing any number other than 50 through 79. Any player wearing 50 through 79 is not permitted to go downfield until the pass is thrown.

The pro rule allows all offensive players who are on either end of the line (other than a center, guard, or tackle) or who are at least one yard behind the line at the snap to go out for a forward pass. The quarterback in a T-formation cannot receive a forward pass in pro ball, but he can in college ball.

What is a complete pass?

A complete pass is one that is caught by a player who is inbounds when he gains possession of the ball.

What is an incomplete pass?

An incomplete pass is one that is not caught—one that hits the ground, one that hits a goal post, or one that goes out of bounds not in player possession.

What is an intercepted pass?

An intercepted pass is one that is caught by a member of the opposing team.

What is a deflected pass?

A deflected pass is one that has its initial direction changed or altered because of some contact by a player of either team.

A forward pass is batted into the air by a defensive player. Are all players eligible to catch the ball and advance?

INTERIOR LINEMAN

SCRIMMAGE LINE

All players on both offense and defense become eligible pass receivers once the pass has been touched by a defensive player. If the ball touches a defensive player and then hits the ground, it is merely an incomplete pass.

A forward pass in flight hits an inbounds official and bounces into the air, where it is caught by an eligible receiver. Is this legal?

This is a perfectly legal play. A pass becomes incomplete when it hits the ground, a goal post, or goes out of bounds not in player possession. Hitting the official is ignored, and the ball continues in play.

What are the ways a forward pass can become incomplete?

In pro ball the following forward passes become incomplete and the ball is dead immediately:

1. A pass that hits the ground or goes out of bounds.
2. A pass that hits the goal post of either team.
3. A pass that is caught by an offensive player after it has touched an ineligible receiver.
4. A pass that is touched by an eligible receiver and is then caught by a second eligible receiver before a defensive man touches the ball.
5. An illegal forward pass that is caught by a member of the passing team.

In college ball the following forward passes become incomplete and the ball is dead immediately:

1. A pass that hits the ground or goes out of bounds.
2. A pass that hits a goal post of either team.
3. A pass that is received by a player who comes down to the ground out of bounds.

On a pass play, a defensive back intercepts the ball on his two-yard line, and his momentum carries him into the end zone, where he is downed. Where will the ball next be put in play?

In both college and pro ball any pass interception on or inside the defensive team's five-yard line is next put into play at the spot of the interception if the interceptor's momentum carries him into his own end zone.

A defensive back intercepts a legal forward pass in his end zone, and while he is in the air his shoulder hits the goal post. What is the ruling?

In college ball it is an incomplete pass. The defensive man did not land in the field of play without going out of bounds first. The goal post is out of bounds in college ball, and so is the pass in this case. In pro ball the touching of the goal post is ignored and the play continues.

A forward pass is batted into the air by a defensive player. It is then batted by an offensive player and caught in flight by still another offensive player, who goes for a touchdown. Is this legal?

In college ball a pass in flight, whether forward or backward, may be batted in any direction in the field or the end zone. The play is perfectly legal and the touchdown counts. The pro rule is slightly different. A pass in flight may be batted anywhere by the defense, but the offense may only bat a pass to prevent an opponent from intercepting the pass. I would have to see the play under pro rules in order to rule on it, but it would most likely be ruled a legal touchdown, in my opinion.

Is it always a touchback when a forward pass is incomplete in the opponent's end zone on fourth down?

In college ball it is never a touchback but merely an incomplete pass, and the defense would get the ball at the spot where the ball was previously snapped.

The pro rule is quite different. When the offensive team is inside their opponents' twenty-yard line and the pass is incomplete in the end zone on fourth down, it is an automatic touchback and the defending team will get the ball on their own twenty-yard line, first and ten.

A forward pass hits an offensive receiver and bounds up into the air. A defensive man dives for the ball and catches it but lands out of bounds. Is this an incomplete pass?

It is definitely an incomplete pass. The defensive man would have had to land with one foot inbounds in college ball and with two feet inbounds in pro ball.

Where does the playing field end and the sideline begin?

The playing field is measured from the inside edges of all the boundary lines, such as sidelines, goal lines, and end lines. The field ends where the sidelines begin; the entire line is out of bounds.

Are all boundary lines out of bounds in all sports?

Some are and some aren't. Football and basketball playing areas are measured from the inside of the boundary lines. The boundary lines are entirely out of bounds. Baseball and tennis playing areas are measured from the outside edge of the boundary lines. The lines in these sports are in play. There are many other examples, but the lesson to be learned is that there is no rule of thumb for the relationship between playing surfaces and boundary lines in sports.

Can two consecutive eligible pass receivers touch a forward pass after it has been touched by a defensive man?

In both college and pro ball, once the defense touches a forward pass anywhere on the field, all offensive players become eligible receivers and any number of offensive men can touch the pass before it is caught.

A forward pass touches an eligible offensive receiver and bounces into the air. It is caught by another eligible offensive receiver, who lands on the sideline. Is this a foul or merely an incomplete pass?

In college ball it is an incomplete forward pass, nothing more. In pro ball it is a foul for a second eligible touching the forward pass. The penalty is loss of the down at the spot where the ball was previously snapped.

A pass receiver catches the ball and lands on the seat of his pants inbounds. Is this a completed pass?

It is a completed pass in both college and pro ball.

A pass receiver catches the ball and lands on his head inbounds. Is this a completed pass?

It is a completed pass in college and pro ball. Only when a receiver comes down on his feet is there a difference in the rules. College ball requires one foot inbounds and pro ball requires both feet inbounds.

How would you describe roughing the passer?

A passer who is standing still or fading backward is obviously out of the play after the ball leaves his hand and must be protected until the pass ends or until he starts to move into a distinctly defensive position. The referee must determine whether the defender had a reasonable chance to stop his momentum during an attempt to block or bat the pass, or tackle the passer while he still had the ball. This call, like many in football, is primarily up to the judgment of the referee.

What is the penalty for roughing the passer?

The penalty is a fifteen-yard walk-off against the defensive team from the spot of the previous snap. If the foul is really flagrant, the offender can be put out of the game. College and pro enforcement is the same.

How long does the passer continue to be protected during a down?

In both college and pro ball the player who throws a legal forward pass is protected from roughing until the pass ends. In other words, he is protected while the pass is in flight.

What is an illegal forward pass?

An illegal forward pass is one that is not made according to the rules.

How many different kinds of illegal forward passes are there?

In pro ball, the following are illegal forward passes:

1. A forward pass after possession has changed. The penalty is five yards from the spot of the pass.

2. A second forward pass from behind the line of scrimmage. The penalty is loss of down at the spot where the ball was previously snapped.

3. A forward pass from beyond the line of scrimmage. The penalty is five yards from the spot of the pass and loss of the down.

In college ball the following are illegal forward passes:

1. The same as condition No. 1 under pro rules, with the same penalty.

2. The same as condition No. 2 under pro rules. The penalty is different, however: a five-yard penalty from the spot of the second pass and loss of the down.

3. The same as condition No. 3 under pro rules, with the same penalty.

4. Intentionally grounding or intentionally throwing a forward pass out of bounds to save a loss of yards or to conserve time. The penalty is five yards from the spot of the pass and loss of the down.

The passer rolls to his right and finally throws a forward pass from beyond the line of scrimmage. What is the ruling?

In both college and pro ball it is an illegal forward pass. This foul calls for a five-yard penalty from the spot of the pass and loss of the down. The enforcement is the same in both pro and college ball.

An illegal forward pass is intercepted by a defensive man who runs for a touchdown. Is this legal?

The run is legal and the touchdown would count, providing the penalty for illegal forward pass is declined.

In the process of scrambling, the quarterback runs past the line of scrimmage and then retreats and throws a forward pass from behind the line of scrimmage. What is the ruling if the pass is complete, incomplete, or intercepted?

This is a perfectly legal play in both college and pro ball. The only restriction during a forward pass play, where the passer is concerned, is that he be on or behind the line of scrimmage when the pass is thrown. He may advance beyond the line and then retreat as long as he is not beyond the line when he releases the ball.

What is the penalty for intentionally grounding a forward pass in one's own end zone?

In college ball it is an automatic safety. Score two points for the defensive team. In pro ball it is a fifteen-yard penalty from the previous line of scrimmage and loss of the down.

Isn't intentional grounding of a forward pass also an illegal forward pass?

It is an illegal forward pass in college ball and carries a five-yard penalty plus loss of the down. In pro ball it is not an illegal forward pass. It carries its own penalty of fifteen yards and loss of the down from the spot where the ball was previously snapped.

"Wow, did that look like intentional grounding! As usual, no flag! Don't those refs know anything?" I'm sure every avid football fan has said the above more than once but, believe it or not, the referee does know what's going on, and he is probably the only one in the "house" who does, when it comes to calling intentional grounding of a forward pass. Ready?

In pro ball it is considered intentional grounding when the ball strikes the ground after the passer throws, tosses, or lobs the ball with a deliberate attempt to prevent a loss of yards by his team. The pro referee can use his own good judgment on this type of play.

The college rule is quite different. If any player is occupying the area into which a forward pass is thrown, even though he may be an ineligible receiver or a defender, it is not to be construed as intentional grounding. College rules leave no room for judgment on grounding situations.

Is it legal to throw two forward passes on the same offensive play?

Only one forward pass may be made during each play from scrimmage in both college and pro ball.

The quarterback drops back to throw, and his pass is batted back into his hands by a defensive lineman. He then throws again for a touchdown. Is this legal?

It is an illegal forward pass in both college and pro ball. It is the second forward pass during the down.

Can a forward pass be thrown on a kickoff?

A team can never throw a forward pass after possession has changed during a down. The rule is the same in both college and pro ball.

Can a team be penalized for pass interference during an illegal forward pass play?

Under the college rules no pass interference fouls will be called on an illegal forward pass play. Defenders can contact opponents and vice versa in an attempt to get to the ball. The pro rules are the same with one exception. On a play when a second forward pass is thrown, even though it is an illegal pass, interference can be called.

The quarterback advances beyond the line of scrimmage and throws a forward pass. A defender pushes an offensive receiver out of the way and intercepts the ball. Is this pass interference?

It is a legal interception in both college and pro ball. No pass interference is called on any illegal forward pass play under the college rules. Pro rules are the same with the exception of the second forward pass from behind the line.

The quarterback throws a short pass complete behind the line, and the receiver throws a second forward pass from behind the line. A defensive back interferes with an eligible receiver downfield. Is it pass interference?

In college ball it is an illegal forward pass by the offense, and there can be no pass interference by either team. In pro ball it is an illegal forward pass, and pass interference can be called. A foul by each team in this situation would result in an offset. The down would be replayed.

Do both feet of a pass receiver have to make contact with the ground inbounds for a forward pass to be complete?

In college ball only one foot must contact the ground inbounds for the pass to be complete. The pro rule requires both feet to be in contact with the ground inbounds in order to have a complete pass. Both college and pro rules are based on the catcher of the pass coming down on his feet. First contact inbounds is sufficient if the receiver comes down on any part of his body other than his feet.

Can a forward pass be complete if the ball is caught outside of a sideline while the receiver's feet are in contact with the ground inbounds?

The position of the ball has no bearing on whether the pass is complete or incomplete. It is the position of the man, and in this play he has qualified for a completion.

A receiver is carried, not knocked, by a defensive back so that his feet come down out of bounds. Is this pass incomplete?

If a receiver is carried out of bounds by a defensive man the pass is ruled complete at the spot where the receiver went out of bounds.

What happens if a pass is caught simultaneously by a receiver and a defender and they both land inbounds or one lands inbounds and one lands out of bounds?

If both players land inbounds the rules award the ball to the passing team. If one man lands in and one lands out, the pass is incomplete.

When a pass receiver is running his pattern and is bumped out of bounds or steps out on his own, can he come back onto the field and make a legal catch of the pass?

Whenever an originally eligible receiver goes out of bounds for any reason he is restricted by rule, both in college and pro ball, from touching the pass until a member of the defending team touches it. In college ball the penalty is loss of the down at the spot where the ball was previously snapped. Pro rules consider it an incompletion.

An eligible receiver goes out of bounds. While he is out of bounds a defensive player touches the pass. The receiver then returns in-bounds to catch the pass. Is this legal?

It is a legal catch because of the touching by the defensive back.

A pass receiver is in his opponents' end zone, and while trying to get away from a defender his foot "ticks" the end line. He catches the pass for a score. Does the score stand?

It is not a score in pro or college ball. This receiver became an ineligible pass receiver when his foot hit the end line.

Do the defending players also have to stay inbounds in order to be able to intercept a pass?

In college ball the defensive team is not required to stay inbounds except on kickoffs. In pro ball a defensive back can run out of bounds to avoid a man and still be eligible to catch the pass, but he must be inbounds at the snap.

An eligible receiver goes out of bounds on his way downfield. He comes back inbounds but does not touch the pass, which is legally completed. Is this a legal play?

It is a perfectly legal play. It would have been a foul if the out-of-bounds player had touched the pass before a defender had touched it.

Is a backward pass treated any differently under the rules than a lateral pass?

They are both the same under college and pro rules. Any pass that does not go forward is considered to have gone backward.

Is a lateral pass treated the same as a forward pass?

A lateral pass becomes a free ball that either team may recover if it is incomplete. A forward pass is dead, and no one may recover when it is incomplete.

Can a lateral or backward pass be recovered and advanced by the defensive team?

In both college and pro ball if a lateral or backward pass is recovered in flight, the defense may advance. If the ball strikes the ground only the offensive team may advance. College ball never allows the defense to pick up a fumble or a muffed lateral or backward pass and advance. Pro rules allow the defense to pick up a fumble and advance, but they do not allow a touched or muffed backward or lateral pass to be advanced, only recovered.

An incomplete backward pass hits the ground and a defensive man picks it up and runs for a touchdown. Is this legal?

In both college and pro ball, the instant the defensive man gains possession of the ball it becomes dead by rule, with no advance allowed.

A backward pass is caught and fumbled by the passing team, and a defensive man picks up the ball and runs with it. Is this legal?

In college ball there is no advance of a grounded fumble by the defensive team. The advance would be perfectly legal under the pro rules.

A backward pass is incomplete or it is caught and fumbled, and any member of the offensive team picks up the ball and advances. Is this a legal advance?

The offensive team can always advance their own fumble or backward pass. College and pro rules are the same in this regard.

A backward pass hits a goal post. Does the ball continue in play, or is it dead by rule?

In pro ball the football touching the goal post is ignored and the ball continues in play. In college ball the ball would be out of bounds in the end zone because the collegiate goal posts are on the end lines and are out of bounds.

A pass is thrown forward by the quarterback, but a strong wind blows the ball back and it lands behind the spot from which it was thrown. What is it?

In pro ball it is an incomplete forward pass. In college ball it is a backward pass, and it is in play for either team to recover. The pro rule uses initial direction as a determining factor, while the college rule is entirely different. The point where the ball first strikes anything determines whether it is a forward or backward pass.

What is forward pass interference?

Forward pass interference is when the movement of any offensive or defensive player beyond the line of scrimmage hinders the progress of any eligible opponent in an attempt to get to the pass. However, any incidental contact that may occur while two or more players are making a bona fide attempt to catch or touch the ball is not considered pass interference.

Is there much judgment on the part of officials where pass interference is concerned?

You can say that again!

Can you have pass interference beyond the line of scrimmage if the pass is completed behind the line?

As long as a pass goes forward, all interference regulations are enforced. The answer is yes.

Can there be pass interference after a ball has been touched by a defensive player?

Player restrictions on forward pass plays are off whenever the ball is touched by either team. There cannot be pass interference once the ball is touched by a defensive or an offensive player anywhere on the field.

Can there be pass interference behind the line of scrimmage?

Pass interference regulations do not include action behind the line of scrimmage. There can be no pass interference behind the line of scrimmage.

What is a pick play?

During a down in which a legal forward pass is thrown, an offensive receiver who is downfield attempts to screen a defensive back but makes contact with him, preventing the defender from covering another legal offensive pass receiver.

Would a foul be called for interference on a forward pass play if a receiver and a defender bump into each other while both are going for the ball?

No interference would be called if both men were making a bona fide effort to get to the ball.

A forward pass is touched by a defensive back, and a moment later the intended offensive receiver is knocked down from behind by another defender, who intercepts the pass. Is this interference?

In both college and pro ball, once the defense touches a legal forward pass, everyone on the field becomes eligible, and there can be no pass interference. The contact by the interceptor is legal unless it is unnecessarily rough.

A screen pass is thrown behind the line of scrimmage, and while the ball is in the air a defensive man uses his hands to push the intended receiver out of the way in order to get to the ball. Is this pass interference?

The ball is free and may be pursued by any player while it is behind the line. Even a forward pass is fair game. There is no pass interference behind the line of scrimmage in pro or college ball, and the defense is allowed to push or pull an opponent out of the way to get to that ball.

A forward pass is touched by an eligible end and is then caught and advanced by another eligible receiver. Is this a legal advance?

In pro ball the advance is not legal and the ball is blown dead. The touching by a second eligible receiver is treated just like an incomplete pass. It is loss of the down at the spot where the ball was previously snapped. In college ball it is a legal advance; any number of eligible receivers may legally touch a forward pass.

What happens if a forward pass accidentally hits an ineligible receiver on or behind the line of scrimmage?

In pro ball the accidental illegal touching by an ineligible receiver behind the line of scrimmage is treated the same as an incomplete pass. It is loss of the down at the spot where the ball was previously snapped. College rules are more severe in the case of illegal touching. If it happens behind the line it is a five-yard penalty and loss of the down.

What if an ineligible receiver intentionally touches or catches a forward pass behind the line of scrimmage?

In pro ball it is a fifteen-yard penalty and loss of the down. In college ball it is exactly the same as accidental touching, a five-yard penalty and loss of the down.

What happens if a forward pass accidentally hits an ineligible receiver who is legally blocking an opponent beyond the line of scrimmage?

Whenever a legal forward pass touches an ineligible receiver who is beyond the line of scrimmage for any reason, the penalty is fifteen yards from the spot where the ball was previously snapped and loss of the down. College and pro rules are the same in this regard.

Once an offensive lineman who is also an ineligible pass receiver makes contact with an opponent on the line of scrimmage during a legal pass play, how far can he legally block the opponent downfield?

In both pro and college ball there is no restriction on the distance a defensive man can be blocked downfield, providing the initial contact is made within a yard of the line of scrimmage by the offensive blocker.

What is the penalty enforcement for forward pass interference by the offense?

In pro and college ball the distance penalty is the same, fifteen yards from the spot where the ball was previously snapped and loss of the down. In college ball, if offensive pass interference occurs in the opponents' end zone, the team that is fouled has an option of the penalty or an awarded touchback. The pros only give the touchback option when it is fourth down inside the five-yard line.

What is the penalty enforcement for forward pass interference by the defense?

In pro and college ball the penalty is the same, first down for the offensive team at the spot of the foul. If the interference is in the end zone, the ball is put on the one-yard line with goal to go.

What restrictions are placed on offensive players during a forward pass play?

In pro ball the center, guards, and tackles are restricted from going beyond the line of scrimmage until the ball leaves the passer's hand and are restricted from blocking beyond their initial line charge until the ball is touched by anyone. The offensive backs are restricted from any blocking beyond the line of scrimmage from the time of the snap until the ball is touched. College rules are exactly the same with one exception. All players who are numbered 50 through 79 are restricted from going downfield until the ball is thrown and from blocking until the ball is touched regardless of their position.

What restrictions are placed on defensive players during a forward pass play?

The defensive team is restricted from contacting or blocking any eligible receiver beyond the line of scrimmage from the time the ball leaves the passer's hand until the ball is touched by any player.

What is an ineligible pass receiver?

An ineligible pass receiver is a member of the offensive team who is restricted by rule from going beyond the line of scrimmage until a forward pass is thrown, or an originally eligible receiver who goes out of bounds during the play (he remains ineligible until a defender touches the ball).

Which offensive players are ineligible receivers?

In pro ball ineligible receivers are linemen who are not on the end of the line, and any who are on the end of the line if they are the center, guards, or tackles. (Centers, guards, and tackles are ineligible even if they are on the end of the line.) The quarterback, who is in a position to receive a hand-to-hand snap from the

center, is also ineligible, along with any eligible receiver who goes
out of bounds during a pass play. In college ball all men who are
numbered 50 through 79 are ineligible, and all other men who are
not on the end of the line or legally in the backfield are ineligible.
In college ball the quarterback is an eligible pass receiver.

**What is the penalty for having an ineligible pass receiver down-
field?**

In both college and pro ball the penalty is fifteen yards from the
spot where the ball was previously snapped.

**The center has no defensive man rushing his position on a pass
play. After he snaps the ball, he charges two yards beyond the
line of scrimmage and blocks the middle linebacker. Is this a
legal block?**

If the pass is thrown forward at any time during the down, the
block is illegal and is also offensive pass interference. The blocking by offensive linemen on pass plays must be within one yard
of the line and must be initiated immediately after the snap.
College and pro rules are the same in this regard.

**The center or any other ineligible receiver has no defensive man
across from him at the snap. He goes three yards downfield and
blocks no one. The pass is thrown incomplete. Was this man
illegally downfield?**

In both college and pro ball the offensive lineman is illegally
downfield.

**Can an ineligible pass receiver legally throw a forward pass
during a down?**

It is possible. In both college and pro ball any offensive player
who is in legal position at the snap can become a passer during

the down. He must be behind the line of scrimmage when the pass is thrown.

Can a forward pass be thrown to an ineligible pass receiver?

The answer is yes. Not only can the pass be thrown to an ineligible receiver, but he may also catch the ball and advance. It is a foul, and if the penalty is accepted the passing team will be penalized fifteen yards and the down will count. College and pro rules are the same in this regard.

The quarterback takes the snap from center, flips the ball to a halfback, and goes downfield for a pass. The pass is never thrown. Is this legal?

In college ball it is perfectly legal for the quarterback to go out for a pass. In pro ball the quarterback, when in position directly behind the center, is an ineligible pass receiver; it is a fifteen-yard penalty from the spot where the ball was previously snapped.

A defensive man intercepts a pass on his six-yard line and he continues on into the end zone, where he is downed. Is this a touchback?

In both college and pro ball it is a safety. Score two points for the passing team.

A defensive man intercepts on his own three-yard line, and his momentum carries him into the end zone. He runs the ball out to the two-yard line, where he is tackled. Where is the ball next put into play?

It is first down for the intercepting team on their two-yard line.

SCORING

It was opening day for Big Ten football, and Utah was visiting the Golden Gophers of Minnesota. The weather was on the warm side, about ninety degrees, but the temperature didn't seem to have much effect on the well-conditioned players.

The game was tied 0–0 at halftime, and the underdog Utah team had a slight statistical edge in total yards gained. Both teams scored in the third quarter, and as time began to run out, Minnesota held a slim 7–6 lead. To the surprise of the Gophers and the crowd of some thirty-five thousand, Utah opened the fourth quarter with a long touchdown pass, and they led 12–7 with only a minute gone in the quarter.

The rest of the fourth quarter was a seesaw battle, with neither team making much headway. Utah punted with only seconds remaining in the game, and Minnesota took over on the fifty-yard line. The clock showed ten seconds left in the ball game. A quick pass advanced the ball to the forty-yard line. Then a time out killed the clock with six seconds remaining. There was time for one last play, and things looked mighty bad for the Gophers.

They broke out of the huddle, and their quarterback took the snap. He faded, scrambled and finally let fly a long lofting pass toward the distant end zone. A lone Minnesota pass receiver was waiting there as the ball started on its downward path. Suddenly the Utah safetyman leaped into the air, high above the Minnesota man, in an attempt to intercept the pass. Why this safetyman chose to intercept instead of just knocking the ball down will never be known, but just before he and the ball returned to the ground in the end zone the Minnesota receiver stole the ball from his grasp, and all of a sudden it was a touchdown and victory for the Gophers. The game had ended on that play, and the final score was Minnesota 13, Utah 12.

TOUCHDOWN

How wide is the goal line?

In pro and college ball the goal line is four inches wide.

Where does the goal line begin?

Each goal line is entirely in the end zone. The inside edge of the line is where the goal line begins.

Is the end zone the same size in college and pro ball?

The end zone is the same size in pro, college, high school, grammar school, and so on. It is ten yards deep and the width of the field.

What is a touchdown?

A touchdown is when a player is legally in possession of the football while any part of the ball is on, above, or behind the opponents' goal line.

What is the point value of a touchdown?

The touchdown is worth six points.

Why is a touchdown six points and not some other evaluation?

You've got me! If any of you football fans have the answer, please let me know. The rules say six points, and that's good enough for me. Years ago, in the late 1800s, a single point was awarded when a touchdown was scored. Somewhere along the line the six points came to be.

What part of a ball carrier governs the ruling on a touchdown?

The ball carrier is not required to be in the end zone for a touchdown to be scored. He can also have part of his body in the end zone and not score a touchdown. It is the ball that scores the touchdown as long as it is in player possession.

How much of the ball must penetrate the goal line on a touchdown?

When any part of the ball is on, above, or behind the goal line, a touchdown is scored providing the ball is in possession of the ball carrier and the goal belongs to the defending team.

Can a touchdown be scored without the ball or the runner touching the ground in the end zone?

The ball only has to break the plane of the goal line. Once it is on or above the goal line in possession, the runner can be driven back into the field of play and it will still be a touchdown.

Can any offensive player score a touchdown?

Any offensive player can score a touchdown providing he got possession of the ball by legal means.

Can any defensive player score a touchdown?

Any defensive player can score a touchdown as long as he got possession of the ball legally.

Does the ball become dead the instant a touchdown is scored?

The answer is yes. You may question a touchdown when the ball carrier crosses the goal line and fumbles, or a pass receiver catches a pass in the end zone and drops it as soon as he is hit, but the rule calls for the ball to be dead the very instant the touchdown is scored. It may not look good to you, but it is. Leave those calls to the officials.

What officials are responsible for determining whether a runner has scored a touchdown on a short running play, pass play, kick-off return, or punt return?

On short runs and goal line plays, the head linesman and the line judge will call the touchdown. On pass plays or long runs it will usually be the back judge or field judge or both, and on kick returns it will be the referee and possibly the head linesman and line judge.

The kicker is back in his end zone. He fumbles or muffs the snap from center, and a defensive man recovers in the end zone. Is it a touchdown?

It is definitely a touchdown. Whenever a fumble is recovered by the defense in their opponents' end zone, a touchdown is scored.

A pass receiver leaps into the air in the end zone and receives a pass, but before he lands he is knocked out of bounds by a defensive back. Is this a touchdown?

This is an incomplete pass. The pass receiver must land inbounds with the ball in his possession in the end zone to score a touchdown.

The ball carrier takes the handoff from the quarterback on his opponents' three-yard line. He drives for the goal line and hits the goal post instead. He is then driven back to the three-yard line. What is the ruling?

This is obviously a pro football question, because the pros have their goal posts on the goal line, while college ball has them on the end line. In pro ball it would be a touchdown. The posts are either on the goal line or recessed into the end zone. In either case, contact with the goal post by the ball carrier would result in a score. In college ball he would have scored long before he got to the goal post. College goal posts are out of bounds.

Is it a touchdown if a receiver catches a pass in the air and alights in the end zone with one foot inbounds and the next step out of bounds?

In college ball it is a touchdown. Only one foot is required to be inbounds at the time of the catch, providing the other foot is in the air. If the receiver came down with one foot inbounds and the other foot out of bounds at the same time, the pass would be incomplete. In pro ball it is an incomplete pass. The pros must land inbounds with both feet.

Is it a touchdown when a pass receiver standing in the end zone is touching the goal post when he receives the ball?

In pro ball it is a touchdown because the goal post is in the end zone. In college ball it is an incomplete pass because the goal post is out of bounds under collegiate rules.

What is the ruling if a forward pass is caught simultaneously by a receiver and a defender in the end zone?

Whenever a forward pass is caught at the same time by opposing players, the ball is awarded to the passing team. It is a touchdown.

A ball carrier is not going to make it to the goal line of his opponents, so he reaches out with the ball at arm's length to break the plane of the goal line. Is it possible to score a touchdown if the runner's body never crosses the goal line?

As long as the ball crosses the plane of the goal line for even an instant, it is a touchdown. The ball carrier had better reach out before the ball is blown dead.

The ball carrier dives over the goal line but loses possession when he hits the ground. Is this a fumble or a touchdown?

The touchdown is scored as soon as the ball enters the end zone. It then becomes dead, and you can't fumble a dead ball.

A runner is stopped on his opponents' one-yard line. One of his teammates pushes him over the goal line. Is it a touchdown?

It is no touchdown. Pushing or pulling a teammate who has the ball in his possession is a foul in both pro and college ball. The penalty in pro ball is fifteen yards from the spot of the foul. The collegiate penalty is five yards from the spot of the foul.

Is it possible to score a touchdown without the clock ever starting?

In college ball the clock starts when a kickoff is legally touched. It is legally touched when a player on the receiving team touches it or when a player on the kicking team touches it after the ball has traveled ten yards. An untouched kickoff that goes into the end zone of the receiving team is an automatic touchback. In college ball it is not possible to score a touchdown without the clock starting.

In pro ball the clock starts on a kickoff when the ball is kicked, except for the last two minutes of the second and fourth quarters. Then the clock starts when the kick is legally touched. If the kicking team recovers an untouched kickoff in the receivers' end zone during these last two minutes, it is a touchdown, and believe it or not, the clock would never have started.

The kickoff is rolling around on the receivers' two-yard line. In an attempt to field the kick, the receiver muffs the ball into his end zone, where a player on the kicking team falls on the ball. Is this a touchdown?

Touchdown! Score six points for the kicking team. In pro ball it would be a touchdown whether the receiver touched the ball or not, since under pro rules a kickoff is anybody's ball once it travels ten yards. In college ball it would be an automatic touchback if the receiver had not muffed or touched the ball.

A defender intercepts a pass on his two-yard line, and his momentum carries him into the end zone. In his attempt to run the ball out of the end zone he fumbles, and the original passing team recovers. Is this a touchdown?

It is a touchdown in both college and pro ball if the ball is recovered in the end zone. If the interceptor had chosen not to run and had downed the ball in the end zone it would have been his team's ball at the spot of the interception: the two-yard line.

A defensive player intercepts in his end zone, and while he is attempting to run the ball out of the end zone the ball is stolen by a passing member of the opposing team. Is this still a touchback?

It is a touchdown. A live ball in player possession can be stolen by either team.

On fourth down, a runner is on his opponents' two-yard line when he fumbles. The ball bounces into the end zone, where it is recovered by the runner. Is this a touchdown?

It is a touchdown in both college and pro ball. However, in pro ball it would not have been a touchdown had any player other than the fumbler recovered the ball. This rule is only in effect on fumbles inside the opponents' ten-yard line on fourth down.

A receiver muffs a kick on the field of play and the ball goes into the end zone, where a player on the kicking team recovers. Is it a touchdown?

Touchdown! Score six points for the kicking team.

Can a touchdown be awarded if the defensive team continually fouls in order to keep their opponents from putting the ball into play?

College and pro rules both provide for an awarded touchdown in the above situation.

TRY FOR POINT

What is meant by a try?

A "try" or a "try for point" is an opportunity given a team that has just scored a touchdown, to score one or two additional points during a single play from scrimmage.

What is an extra point?

This is a term often used instead of "try" or "try for point." It has the exact same meaning as the try.

Can you use an artificial or natural tee on a try for point?

In college ball an artificial or natural tee may be used on a try, providing it does not elevate the ball more than two inches from the ground. The pro rules do not allow a tee of any kind to be used on a try for point.

When does a try for point begin and when does it end?

The try for point is a very special play in football. It actually has its own set of rules, which in many ways are contrary to the basic rules of the game. In both college and pro ball the try begins when the referee blows his whistle and gives the ready-for-play signal (a chopping motion of the hand and arm in a downward direction). The try ends when it is successful, when an attempted kick is obviously not good or when an attempted run or pass is unsuccessful in getting the ball across the goal line. It also ends when the defense gains possession of the ball during the down.

How much time does a team have to put the ball into play for the try for point after they score their touchdown?

After the touchdown has been scored, the officials quickly unpile the players if it is necessary. They give the teams a reasonable amount of time to get ready and to substitute. When this is done the ready-for-play signal is given by the referee and the count begins. In pro ball the offense has thirty seconds to snap the ball after the ready-for-play signal has been given. In college ball the offense has only twenty-five seconds to snap the ball.

When is a team eligible to attempt a try for point?

Only after they have scored a touchdown.

Can a team score two points on a try for point?

In college ball a team can score one or two points on a try, depending upon the method of scoring they use. One point is scored if the ball is place kicked or drop kicked through the goal posts and higher than the crossbar. Two points are scored if the ball crosses the opponents' goal line by a run or completed pass. In pro ball a successful kick, run, or completed pass all score one point on a try for point.

Why can college teams score two points on a try when pro teams can only score one point?

The American Football League used to have a two-point try before it merged with the National Football League. Why they did away with it is a mystery to me. College rules put the two-point try into the game to eliminate ties and to add a little more excitement to the game.

With the score 7–0 late in the game, a recovered fumble or an intercepted pass puts the losing team within scoring range. Everyone in the stands, the viewing audience, or the listening audience is asking the same question. If they score a touchdown, will they go for a two-point try and victory? Many teams take the tie by kicking the point but every once in a while some "go for broke" coach decides he'd rather lose than tie, and he goes for the two. This is real excitement.

On what yard line is the ball placed for the try for point?

In pro football the try for point is attempted from the defending team's two-yard line, usually in the middle of the field. In college ball the try is attempted from the three-yard line, usually in the middle of the field.

Can a team request that the ball be placed behind the yard line designated for the try for point?

The ball may be placed on any yard line requested by the offensive team, providing it is no closer than the designated yard line: the two-yard line in pro ball and the three-yard line in college ball.

A team scores a touchdown and requests that their try for point be from the four-yard line instead of the two-yard line. The kick is good, but the offense is offside. From what point is the penalty enforced?

The request to move the ball back is legal, but the penalty will be enforced from the four-yard line instead of the two.

Must the ball be placed in the middle of the field on a try for point?

In both college and pro ball the team attempting the try for point can have the ball placed anywhere between the inbounds lines. Unless a request is made, the ball is always placed in the middle of the field.

Must the ball be kicked on a try for point?

In both college and pro ball the try can be made by kicking, running, or passing the ball according to the rules.

Can a punt be used on a try for point?

In both pro and college ball a punt can definitely be used on a try for point. However, it will not score any points even if it goes through the goal posts. It is not an illegal kick, it just can't be used to score any points. Only a drop kick or a place kick can score points on tries and field goal attempts.

Can the defensive team score on a try for point?

The try for point is a truly unique part of football. It is completely one-sided. Only the team that puts the ball in play can score.

Are the kicker and the holder provided with the same protection on a try as they are on a scrimmage kick?

The kicker and the holder of a place kick are protected from being hit or blocked by the defense until they have had a reasonable opportunity to regain their balance after the kick has been made. This holds true for all place kicks, including tries.

In an attempt to score two points, the offensive team throws a forward pass that is intercepted by the defensive team. Can he return the ball and score the two points that the defense was trying to score?

The instant the pass is intercepted the try is over and the ball is dead by rule. No advance by the interceptor is possible in both college and pro ball.

The offensive team fumbles on a try for point, the defensive team recovers the fumbled ball in the air, and runs the length of the field for a touchdown. How many points are scored?

A big ZERO. No points can be scored by the defensive team on a try for point. As soon as the defensive team gains possession of the ball, the play is over. In both pro and college ball the defensive team can always advance a fumble that is recovered in the air, except on a try for point.

If the defensive team is offside on a successful try, is it possible to accept the penalty and then attempt to run the ball to score two points?

In pro ball you can only score one point on a try. The penalty would be declined, and the point would be good. The ball would be kicked off from the scoring team's forty-yard line.

In college ball the penalty can be accepted and the down replayed from the 1½-yard line. This would put the offensive team in good position to score two points on the try. This is a gamble because they have already scored one point, and by accepting the penalty and going for two points they lose the successful try. If their attempt is unsuccessful from the 1½-yard line they get no points.

A defensive player commits a personal foul on a successful try for point. Where is the enforcement spot for the penalty?

In pro ball the try is good and the penalty is enforced on the kickoff. The scoring team would ordinarily kick off from their own forty-yard line, but when you walk off the fifteen-yard penalty against the fouling team it would put the ball on the receivers' forty-five-yard line for the kickoff.

In college ball the scoring team has two options. They can accept the successful try and have the penalty enforced on the kickoff, or they can replay the down with half the distance enforcement of the penalty and attempt a two-point try.

What fouls are considered personal fouls?

Some of the more well-known personal fouls are as follows: striking with the fists; kicking; kneeing; striking on the head, neck, or face with the heel, back, or side of the hand, wrist, forearm, elbow, or clasped hands; spearing; piling; and several more.

An offensive player is offside on a try for point, and the kick or run is good. How do you enforce the penalty?

In both college and pro ball, if the penalty was accepted enforcement would be from the spot where the ball was previously snapped. The down would then be replayed. If the penalty was declined by the defensive team the try would be successful.

If the offensive team commits forward pass interference on a try for point, from what point would the penalty be enforced?

There would be no distance penalty in this situation. The try would be over and no points could be scored by the offensive team. Offensive pass interference is usually a fifteen-yard penalty from the spot where the ball was previously snapped plus loss of the down. On a try the loss-of-down penalty would automatically nullify any points or any chance for a replay.

During the try for point the offense fumbles the ball into the end zone and the defensive team intentionally kicks the ball out of the end zone to keep the offensive team from recovering it. Is this a foul? If it is, from what point would the penalty be enforced?

In both college and pro ball the act of illegally kicking a free ball is a foul. In pro ball, if the foul actually kept the offense from recovering the ball in the end zone, the point would be awarded. Otherwise the down would be replayed and the offense would be given another chance for a successful try.

In college ball the illegal kick would result in a safety. Score one point for the offensive team. A safety always scores two points except if it happens on a try for point; then it always scores one point. This is also true in pro ball.

The defensive team is called for pass interference on a try for point. What is the penalty?

If the try is good, the penalty will be declined. If the try is unsuccessful and the penalty is accepted, the ball will be placed on the one-yard line and the down will be replayed. The penalty for defensive interference in the field of play is first down at the spot of the foul.

A try for point is attempted by a drop kick or a place kick, but it is blocked. Can the kicking team recover the ball behind the line of scrimmage and attempt to make the try by running, passing, or kicking it again?

In college and pro ball the try is over and the ball is dead by rule whenever it is obvious that an attempted kick will not go through the goal posts. The instant the initial kick is blocked, the play is over. If this play was a field goal attempt it could be recovered and play would continue. As I said before, the try is a special part of football, with its own special rules.

If time expires during a touchdown play, is the try for point allowed?

The try for point is a scrimmage play awarded to a team that scores a touchdown. It is an untimed down, and even if time has expired in a quarter or the game, the try is always allowed.

On a try that is not kicked, a safety is scored against the defensive team. How many points would be awarded?

In both college and pro ball a safety scored on a try for point is worth one point for the offensive team.

If both teams foul during a try, what happens?

When both teams foul during a try for point, the down is replayed from the spot where the ball was previously snapped.

If time expires on the touchdown play and both teams foul during the try, what would result?

In both college and pro ball the try would be replayed. If both teams foul on the last timed down of a quarter or the game, the quarter or the game would be over. Only a try has this special rule.

Do all pass regulations remain in force during a try for point?

In both pro and college ball pass regulations remain the same throughout the game, including the try for point.

If a kicked ball hits an upright or the crossbar on a try and it bounces over or through the goal posts, is the point awarded?

The kick is good providing it did not touch the ground or a member of the kicking team before it went through the goal posts.

FIELD GOAL

How is a field goal scored?

In pro ball a field goal is scored when a place kick or a drop kick is made and the entire ball passes through the uprights and over the crossbar of the defensive team's goal posts before it touches the ground or a member of the kicking team. College rules are the same, but with one exception. The ball is only required to pass directly over an upright. This gives the college kicker a little more of a chance at a successful field goal.

A field goal scores how many points?

In pro and college ball a field goal scores three points.

How is the length of a successful field goal determined?

In pro ball the field goal is measured from the spot where it was kicked to the goal posts that it passes through. In college ball the kick is measured from the spot of the kick to the goal posts, even though the college goal posts are on the end line, ten yards behind the goal line.

THE PLACE KICK

Is it permissible to use a tee on a field goal attempt?

In college ball a tee may be used on a field goal attempt, providing it is not more than two inches above ground level. In pro ball a tee cannot be used on field goals.

How many offensive men can be on the line of scrimmage during a field goal attempt?

In pro and college ball there must be at least seven men on the line. The maximum number would be ten linemen if the field goal attempt was a drop kick. If a place kick is used the maximum number of linemen is nine.

Must the ball be kicked once a team lines up for a field goal attempt?

A team can always fake a field goal.

The holder of a field goal attempt usually has one knee on the ground when he receives the ball. Can he get up and run or pass?

He can get up and run or pass in both college and pro ball. Pro rules always allow a runner to get up from the ground if he was not contacted or knocked down by an opponent. College rules do not allow this privilege except when the holder of a place kick has a knee on the ground when he receives the snap. He can get up and run or pass.

On a field goal attempt the holder fumbles the ball, and while the ball is free and rolling on the ground, the kicker kicks the ball and it goes between the goal posts. Is the field goal good?

In both college and pro ball it is an illegally kicked ball. The field goal would not count. The penalty in pro ball is fifteen yards from the spot of the foul. The collegiate penalty is the loss of the ball at the spot of the foul, which means that the defensive team would be given the ball at the spot of the illegally kicked ball.

Is it possible to score a field goal with a drop kick?

College and pro rules both state that a field goal may be made by a place kick or a drop kick. Although you hardly ever hear about drop kicks except in the comic strips, they are legal under all football rules. A drop kick is a kick by a player who drops the ball and kicks it as it touches the ground or as it is rising from the ground.

Can the ball be punted on a field goal attempt?

It can be punted, but a punt can't score points in American football. Canadian football awards one point when a ball is punted across the opponents' goal line. This is called "rouge."

Who rules on the field goal?

In college and pro ball the field judge and the back judge each position themselves behind an upright, and they are solely responsible for ruling whether the kick is high enough and through the uprights.

After a successful field goal, where is the ball put into play?

If there are no penalties, the ball is put into play on the twenty-yard line, first down and ten for the team that was scored upon.

After an unsuccessful field goal attempt, where will the ball be put into play?

In pro ball, if the kick hits a goal post or goes out of the end zone, or is downed by a receiver in the end zone, it is a touchback and the ball will be put into play on the receivers' twenty-yard line. If the ball is caught or fielded in the end zone or in the field, the ball will be put into play wherever it is blown dead after the return. In college ball the rule is the same except for a kick that hits in the end zone untouched by a receiver. This is an automatic touchback, and the next play will be from the twenty-yard line.

A field goal attempt hits the helmet of an offensive lineman and goes between the goal posts. Is the attempt good?

The field goal is no good by rule. A field goal that hits the ground or a member of the kicking team is ruled no good even though the kick meets all other requirements.

A field goal attempt is partially blocked by a defensive man who is behind or beyond the line of scrimmage. The ball goes between the uprights and over the crossbar. Is the kick good?

The kick is good in pro and college ball. A field goal is good if it goes between the goal posts unless it hits the kicking team or the ground first. Touching a defensive man has no effect on the kick according to the rules.

On a field goal attempt the ball passes between the goal posts but the wind blows it directly back between the goal posts and it lands in front of the goal line. Is the kick good or is the ball in play?

The kick is not good but the ball is in play. It can be recovered and advanced by the receiving team. It can be downed by the kicking team, but the ball would then be awarded to the receivers at the spot of the recovery.

On a field goal attempt the ball passes between the goal posts, but the wind blows it back outside of the upright or it blows back under the crossbar. What happens?

In college and pro ball the kick would be good. Score three points for the kicking team.

Is it permissible for a defensive player to climb onto the shoulders of a teammate in an attempt to block a field goal attempt?

In college ball a defensive man cannot be on a teammate's shoulders at the time of the snap. Once the ball is snapped it is legal to climb onto the shoulders of a teammate. In pro ball it is also a foul for defensive players to jump on, stand on, or be picked up by a teammate in an attempt to block a kick.

On a field goal attempt a defensive player is standing in front of the crossbar of the goal posts. He jumps up as the ball arrives and knocks it into the air. The ball is caught by the kicking team in the end zone. What is the ruling?

In collegiate ball it would be a touchdown for the kicking team. Any time a kick is touched in flight in the end zone by the receiving team it becomes a free ball. In pro ball it would be the kickers' ball. Because the goal posts are on the goal line in pro ball, the ball would probably be recovered by the kicking team in the field of play instead of the end zone. It would not result in a touchdown.

Does a blocked field goal attempt that goes beyond the line of scrimmage belong to the team that recovers it?

Unless the ball is touched by a receiver beyond the line of scrimmage, the kickers cannot recover and keep the ball. It would be awarded to the receivers at the spot of recovery. A blocked kick that crosses the line of scrimmage is treated the same as a regular punt that is untouched behind the line before it crosses.

On a field goal attempt the ball strikes an upright and then hits the crossbar. It either goes over the crossbar or it bounces back toward the kicker and hits the ground. What is the ruling?

In both college and pro ball the kick is good if it rebounds between the goal posts. It is dead by rule if it does not go through. Any kick that hits the opponents' goal post that does not score a field goal or a try is dead by rule.

On a field goal attempt the ball deflates in the air before it gets to the goal posts. The "very" soft ball hits the crossbar and sticks there. What is the ruling?

If I were the referee I would call for a new football and replay the down. I hope it never happens.

A field goal attempt is blocked and recovered by the offense behind the line of scrimmage. Can the offense throw a forward pass?

A forward pass can be thrown in both college and pro ball. The only restriction is that the pass be the only forward pass thrown during the down and that it be thrown from behind the line of scrimmage.

If a field goal attempt is blocked behind the line of scrimmage, can the kicking team advance the ball?

The kicking team can always advance a recovered blocked kick from behind the line, even on a try for point.

If a field goal attempt is blocked behind the line of scrimmage, can a defensive man recover and advance the ball?

A blocked kick behind the line of scrimmage can be advanced by the defensive team whether it is picked up from the ground or caught in the air (the exception would be a blocked try for point).

A field goal attempt falls short and hits the ground in the end zone before touching a player. Can a player on the receiving team run with the ball?

In pro ball the player on the receiving team can run with it or he can choose to down the ball in the end zone for a touchback. In college ball when a free kick or a scrimmage kick lands in or bounces into the end zone before it is touched by a receiver, it is an automatic touchback. No runback is possible.

Can a player on the receiving team signal for and make a fair catch on an unsuccessful field goal attempt?

A field goal attempt is a scrimmage kick, and so is a punt. Both kicking situations have the same rules, with the exception of scoring ability. A fair catch signal is perfectly legal on a field goal attempt.

TOUCHBACK

What is a touchback?

Whenever the football is out of bounds behind the defending team's goal line or is blown dead in the defending team's end zone it is a touchback *unless* the force that put the ball into the defender's end zone comes from a defender. A touchback scores no points and the ball is awarded to the team defending that goal at their own twenty-yard line, first and ten.

Where is the ball next put into play when a team is awarded a touchback?

Unless there is a penalty enforcement, the ball will be put in play on the twenty-yard line of the team awarded the touchback. The ball must be put in play by a snap from center.

After a touchback, must the ball be put in play from the middle of the field?

The ball must be snapped from the twenty-yard line anywhere between the hashmarks. The ball is always placed in the middle of the field unless there is a request for a different spot by the offensive team captain.

A defensive back intercepts a pass on the goal line and elects to run, but he is chased back into the end zone, where he is tackled. Is this a touchback or a safety?

If the defensive back intercepts on the goal line, then he is actually in the end zone, and as long as he doesn't run back into the field of play he does not have to worry about a safety. The force that put the ball into the end zone came from the pass. The play is ruled a touchback.

A runner is close to his opponents' end zone when the ball pops out of his hand and bounces into the end zone, where it is recovered by the defense. Is this a touchback?

Yes, it is a touchback. The force that put the ball in the defenders' end zone came from the fumble by the ball carrier.

An offensive player is on his opponents' two-yard line when he fumbles and the ball hits the corner flag or pylon at the intersection of the goal line and the sideline. What is the ruling?

It is a touchback. The corner flag or pylon is out of bounds in the end zone. The force came from the fumble.

A defensive back intercepts a forward pass on his own three-yard line, and his momentum carries him into the end zone. He then runs out of the end zone into the field of play and is tackled on the five-yard line. Shouldn't this be a touchback?

It could never be a touchback, even if the interceptor had remained in the end zone. The ball belongs to the intercepting team at their five-yard line. If the defensive back had stayed in the end zone, the ball would have been put in play on the three-yard line, the spot of the interception.

If a defensive back intercepts a pass in his own end zone and attempts to return the ball but is tackled before he can get out of the end zone, what should the ruling be: a touchback or a safety?

The ruling is a touchback. The determining factor in touchback and safety situations is "impetus" or force. In other words, who is responsible for the ball being in the end zone. In this case, the pass supplied the force, and as long as the defensive man remains in the end zone with the ball in his possession it is a touchback. His successful attempt to run out of the end zone has no bearing on the play. This type of play is very often confused with a safety situation.

A kicked ball strikes the corner flag or pylon at the intersection of the sideline and the goal line. Is the ball out of bounds?

The ball is definitely out of bounds in the end zone. If the kick were made from the field of play, it would be a touchback. If the kick were made from the end zone, it would be a safety.

A punt or kickoff hits the ground in the receivers' end zone and rebounds back onto the field of play and then rolls out of bounds on the one-yard line. Where will the ball next be put in play?

In pro ball the one-yard line will be the next line of scrimmage. In college ball it would be an automatic touchback unless the receivers touched the ball before it hit the end zone.

A kickoff is bounding near the receiving team's three-yard line. In an attempt to pick up the ball, the receiver muffs it into his end zone, where he falls on it. Is this a safety?

This is a touchback. The muff added no new force to the ball. The kick still supplied the force that put the ball in the receiver's end zone.

The receiver of a punt catches the ball in his end zone, and in an attempt to run the ball, he steps on the sideline while still in the end zone. Would this be a safety?

It would be a touchback. The punt put the ball into the end zone, and even though the receiver ran out of bounds in the end zone it is a touchback. The punt was the force.

An offensive player is running for a touchdown when a defensive man knocks the ball out of his hands and the ball bounces into the defenders' end zone, where it is recovered by a defender. What is it?

A touchback. The force that made the ball go into the end zone is considered to be from the offensive player's fumble. The action by the defensive player is ignored.

A player on the receiving team attempts to catch a kick in the field of play. The ball bounces off his hands and goes into his end zone, where another player on the receiving team recovers the ball. Is this a touchback or a safety?

A touchback. No new force is added by the attempted catch of the kick.

In an attempt to stop his kick from going into the opponents' end zone, a player on the kicking team dives on the ball at the three-yard line. With the ball in his grasp he slides into the end zone. Where is the ball next put in play?

In pro ball this play would be ruled a touchback. Whenever a member of the kicking team touches and recovers a scrimmage kick on or inside of the opponents' five-yard line and then carries the ball into the end zone, it is a touchback by rule. In college ball the next play would be snapped from the three-yard line. The ball would be blown dead the instant the player on the kicking team possessed it on the three-yard line.

SAFETY

What is a safety?

If the defending team is responsible for the ball being in their own end zone and it goes out of bounds or is dead in their possession, it is a safety and scores two points for the other team. The defending team must also kick off from their own twenty-yard line after the points are awarded to their opponents. A safety is a very severe situation in football. Not only does the team lose two points, they must give the ball right back to their opponents with a chance for good field position.

How is the ball next put into play after a safety?

The ball must be put in play with a free kick from the twenty-yard line. The kick can be made by a place kick, drop kick, or a punt. A free kick following a safety is the only free kick that is allowed to be a punt.

Doesn't the team that scores in football always kick off after they score?

They usually kick off, but in the case of a safety the scoring team becomes the receiving team on the next kickoff.

The kicker is in his own end zone waiting for the snap from center. The snap is a "boomer," and it goes way over the kicker's head and out of the end zone. Is it a safety?

It is a safety. The impetus or force that made the ball go out of the kicker's end zone came from the kicking team's snap from center. This factor determines touchback or safety.

A short punt from the kicking team's end zone strikes the ground beyond the line of scrimmage and bounces back toward the kickers' end zone. The ball is recovered in the end zone by the kicker. What is the ruling?

It is a safety. The force that put the ball in the kicker's end zone came from his kick.

A punt from the kicker's end zone hits a member of the receiving team beyond the line of scrimmage, and the ball rebounds back and out of the kicking team's end zone. Is it a safety?

A safety it is. The kicked ball supplied the force that put it out of the kicker's end zone, even though it hit a receiver. Remember, a kick is still a kick until it is possessed by a player, goes out of bounds, or is blown dead by the officials.

The offensive team punts from their end zone. The kick is blocked and goes out of the end zone. Where is the ball next put into play?

The result of the play is a safety. Score two points for the receiving team. The ball will next be free kicked from the kicker's twenty-yard line.

A member of the receiving team catches a kickoff on his own ten-yard line and immediately throws a backward pass to a teammate who is standing on his five-yard line. The pass is muffed and rolls into the end zone, where a player on the receiving team falls on the ball. What is the ruling?

This is a safety. The kick ended when it was caught by the receiver. The backward pass supplied the force that put the ball into the receivers' end zone. If the kicking team had recovered, it would be a touchdown.

The receiver of a kickoff catches the ball on his two-yard line, and in his attempt to advance is forced to take a route back into his end zone. A member of the kicking team tackles him in the end zone. Is this a touchback?

This is a safety. The player on the receiving team carried the ball into the end zone under his own power. He supplied the force.

A player on the receiving team catches a kick in his end zone. In his attempt to run the ball out, he is downed, with the front of the football touching the goal line. Where will the ball be put into play on the next down?

It will be first down for the receiving team on their own twenty-yard line. The receiver did not get the ball out of the end zone, and since the force that put the ball in the end zone was from the kick, the play is ruled a touchback. In order to get the ball out of the end zone the entire ball must be in the field of play.

A punt from the kicker's end zone, in pro football, hits the goal post and goes out of the kicker's end zone. What is the ruling?

It is a safety. The force came from the kick, not the post.

In pro ball, a punt from the kicker's end zone hits the goal post and is then recovered by a defensive man in the end zone. What is it?

A touchdown. The goal posts are in play in this situation.

The punter is deep in his end zone. He receives the snap from the center, and his foot just "ticks" the end line before he boots the ball. Would the referee ignore this slight contact with the end line?

Absolutely not! The instant the kicker's foot "ticks" that end line with the ball in his possession, the play is over. Score two points for the other team. It is a safety.

During a punt attempt from his own end zone, the kicker misses the ball with his foot, and as the ball hits the ground it is recovered by a defensive player. Safety?

Touchdown! This is the same as a fumbled ball. The defense has recovered a free ball in their opponents' end zone for a touchdown.

During a punt from his own end zone, the ball slides off of the kicker's foot and goes out of bounds behind his goal line. Safety?

Safety is correct. The kick failed to get out of the end zone, and the force that put the ball into the end zone at the start of the play came from the snap.

A player on the receiving team catches a punt on his own two-yard line, and his momentum carries him into his end zone, where he is tackled. Is this a touchback?

This is a safety. It is the receiver who carried the ball into his own end zone, and since he supplied the force, a safety is awarded to the kicking team.

Where would the ball next be put in play when after a snap from center a ball carrier makes contact with a corner flag or a pylon while running out of the end zone?

It would be a safety, and the ball would be free kicked from the twenty-yard line. The flag or pylon at the intersection of the goal line and sideline is out of bounds in the end zone. The runner failed to get the ball out of his end zone. The snap was the force.

The ball is snapped from a team's own five-yard line. The runner is tackled for a loss, and the tip of the ball is touching the goal line when the play is over. What is the ruling?

The ruling is a safety. The snap put the ball into the ball carrier's end zone, and he did not get the entire ball out of the end zone.

A ball carrier is advancing the ball on his own three-yard line when he fumbles. The ball hits a defensive man and bounces into the end zone, where the original ball carrier recovers. Is this a safety?

A safety is scored. The force that put the ball into the ball carrier's end zone came from the fumble. The touching of the ball by the defensive team doesn't affect the original force.

A runner is on his own two-yard line when he fumbles and the ball hits a defensive man and goes out of the end zone. Touchback or safety?

Safety. The force was from the fumble, not the defensive man.

The quarterback passes from his own end zone. The ball hits an ineligible lineman, who is also in the end zone, in the back. What is the ruling?

In pro ball it is merely treated as an incomplete pass. In college ball it is an illegal touching foul; the penalty is a five-yard walk-off from the spot of the previous snap, and the down would count.

The quarterback throws a backward pass from his own three-yard line, and a defensive player bats the ball in flight out of the end zone. Would this be a touchback or a safety?

This would be a safety. The force is from the backward pass in flight. The "actual" force is obviously from the defensive man's batting of the ball, but under the rules a backward pass in flight supplies the force.

The quarterback passes from his end zone to an ineligible lineman who is in the end zone, and the lineman drops the ball. What is the ruling?

In college ball it is illegal touching of a forward pass, a five-yard penalty from the spot of the previous snap, and loss of the down. In pro ball it is a fifteen-yard penalty from the spot of the previous snap and loss of the down.

A forward pass is intercepted in the defenders' end zone. The interceptor then throws an illegal forward pass that is incomplete. From what point is the penalty enforced?

In college and pro ball it is a safety. The enforcement spot is the spot of the pass, and since it is in the end zone, it becomes an automatic safety. If the penalty is declined it is still a safety.

The quarterback throws a backward pass from his own five-yard line. The ball bounces off the hands of the intended receiver and goes out of the end zone. Touchback or safety?

Safety. The pass is the force.

The ball carrier attempts a backward pass, which rolls into his own end zone. While the ball is rolling in the end zone, an offensive man bats the ball out of the end zone to keep the defense from recovering the ball. Safety or touchback?

In college and pro ball the illegal batting in the end zone would result in a safety. Score two points for the defensive team.

GENERAL

One of the greatest "catches" in pro football history occurred on a dreary fall day many years ago. I can't recall who the Washington Redskins were playing that day, but it really doesn't matter.

It was late in the fourth quarter when Sammy Baugh, the great Redskin quarterback, faded to throw one of his patented "bombs." His wide receiver raced down the sidelines with a defensive back in hot pursuit. It looked like an ordinary pass play up to this point. The official covering the area of concern was the back judge, and he was in perfect position to cover the play.

The ball was airborne now, and as it sailed downfield, the offensive receiver cut to the inside, tripped, and fell. The defensive back was coming fast and fell over the fallen Redskin. Both men were out of the play, but the ball kept coming. The "lonely" back judge realized that the pass would land thirty yards beyond the nearest ballplayer.

Now, this great official with a sense of humor second to none did the only thing he could possibly do to avoid chasing the overthrown pass. He darted back some eight or nine yards, leaped into the air, and made a fantastic one-hand catch of the fifty-yard pass. He "brought down the house." The sixty-five thousand fans were on their feet thundering their approval. They had seen one of the finest catches of all time, and it wouldn't even be recorded for posterity. It is for that reason that I mention it now.

How can I get my wife interested in football?

You have taken the first step by purchasing this book. Now give her time to read it, and then take her to a couple of ball games. It won't take long if you make a sincere effort.

What do you think of allowing a range such as the following of points for scoring field goals?

0 to 20 yards	2 points
21 to 30 yards	3 points
31 to 40 yards	4 points
41 and farther	5 points

Every once in a while someone comes up with an idea to revolutionize football. What's wrong with the game as it is? The points awarded for field goals, in my opinion, are more than adequate. If a graduated scale of points were instituted, you would have nothing but field goal attempts. I would personally like to see a reduction in the number of field goals and more emphasis put on scoring touchdowns.

What is the lowest possible winning score in a football game?

In college ball a forfeit results in a 1–0 score. To my knowledge pro football has no provision for a forfeiture.

What happens if the coin lands on its side in the grass, on the toss of the coin?

The toss would be repeated if the coin landed on its side. To avoid this, most referees catch the coin while it is still in the air.

Who would take over if the head coach were to become ill prior to a ball game?

This happens once in a while, and the chief assistant coach usually takes over the ball club.

Do they ever cancel a football game because of bad weather?

It is a very rare happening. I have officiated games in the worst weather imaginable with never a thought of canceling on the part of the game authorities. It would almost take a national emergency to cancel a major college or pro football game.

Can a player score a touchdown for the opposing team?

If a player carries the ball across his own goal line where he is tackled or goes out of bounds, it is a safety. It is not possible to score a touchdown for the other team under these circumstances.

What is the "belly series"?

The quarterback holds the ball to the runner's belly for a second before handing it to him, or pulling it back to hand to another back. The quarterback can also keep the ball and run with it. All the backs have to pretend that they have the ball. It can be very deceptive, and at times a TV cameraman gets faked out in his attempt to follow the ball.

What is the "statue of liberty" play?

The quarterback fades to throw a pass with his arm cocked near his head. A teammate runs behind him and takes the ball and runs with it. This play was more popular years ago.

What is a "look-out block"?

An offensive lineman misses his block on a pass play. As the defensive rusher charges toward the unprotected quarterback, the offensive lineman turns in the direction of the quarterback and yells, "LOOK OUT!!!"

What do the sportcasters and sportswriters mean when they refer to "bench strength"?

They are referring to the amount of football skill possessed by the substitutes.

Is the chain crew always on the same side of the field for both halves of a football game?

In college ball the chain crew is always on the same side of the field. They are always facing the press box. In pro ball the chain crew works one half on each side of the field. However, if both benches are on the same side of the field the chain crew will operate on the side opposite the benches during the entire game.

Can a game be shortened because of darkness?

In pro ball, if the referee is of the opinion that the game will be hindered because of darkness, he may shorten the playing time. If this is done prior to the game, all four periods must be of the same length. During an intermission, the referee can, with the consent of both coaches, shorten the time of any remaining period of periods, if darkness is a problem. In college ball, playing time may be shortened before the start of a game by mutual agreement of the opposing field captains. It may also be shortened by the referee if he feels that darkness will interfere with the game. In either case, all four periods must be of equal length. The playing time of any remaining period or periods can be shortened any time during the game by mutual agreement of the captains and the referee.

Was the football played in the "good old days" a lot tougher and rougher than the football of today? In the old days there was little or no substituting. Players went both ways and usually played the entire game. Equipment was inferior by today's standards and training techniques were pretty basic. The players just had to be supertough. What do you think?

Sports fans have been trying to compare athletes from different eras for as long as I can remember. Would Dempsey have beaten Louis? Would Jim Thorpe have been able to make a modern-day

Olympic team? Could Babe Ruth have hit sixty homers in today's game? These are wonderful questions, and although they will never be answered, they create the interest and discussion that make sports such an important part of our society. My own opinion is that the football of today is rougher and tougher than at any time in its history. The players are bigger and stronger and in top-flight condition at all times. In the "old days" players were weary from playing the entire game, but today, with so much change in game personnel, everyone is ready to give his all on every play. Football is a science, and its complicated plays make it exciting from start to finish.

Is there an avenue open for protest in football games?

To my knowledge organized football has no provision for protest. There have been many historic games where protest would certainly have been lodged had it been possible. The nature of the game, with its hundreds of separate decisions, makes protest impossible. Only 50 percent of the fans and players are satisfied with each decision made by the officials. By the end of a game, no one is satisfied.

Can a penalty be declined?

Any penalty may be declined by the offended team in both pro and college ball.

Which players have the right to discuss penalty options with the officials, and can the coach be consulted before a decision is made on the field?

Only the designated team captain or captains can discuss penalty options with the referee. The coach may not be consulted.

If two players on the offensive team commit fouls on the same play, would you penalize for one or both of the fouls?

Only one penalty would be enforced. If more than one foul is committed by the same team during a down, the defensive captain is given his choice of the foul to be enforced. This rule is the same in both college and pro ball.

What is spearing or piling?

Illegally using the head or helmet to blast into an opponent after his momentum has stopped.

What is the "half the distance" penalty enforcement?

Whenever a penalty will move the ball more than half the actual distance to the nearest goal line, the "half the distance" enforcement is used. Examples: (1) The offense is on their opponents' eight-yard line, and a five-yard penalty is called on the defense. Instead of putting the ball on the three-yard line, it is put "half the distance," to the four-yard line. (2) The offense is on their own twenty-eight-yard line and a fifteen-yard penalty is called against the offense. The ball will be moved back to the fourteen-yard line instead of the thirteen-yard line.

Does any level of football have a ten-yard penalty? Has there ever been a ten-yard penalty, and if not, why?

My sources only go back seventy years, and they tell me that there has never been a ten-yard penalty in football. I have never been able to find a reason for this. The rules call for five and fifteen yards, and that's good enough for me. However, if a team is on its twenty-yard line and a fifteen-yard penalty is called at the twenty-yard line, the "half-the-distance" enforcement would result in a ten-yard penalty. The same situation would result at the other end of the field with the defensive team fouling.

Isn't it an infraction of the rules if a player slams the football to the ground after scoring a touchdown?

The college rule states that after a score or at any time the player in possession must return the ball to an official. The excitement of scoring sometimes causes college players to throw the ball to the ground. If it is the official's opinion that it was not done deliberately, the act is usually not penalized, but the player is given a warning. The pro rules do not restrict this display of excitement.

When a fight occurs on the field and both teams get involved, who gets penalized and what is the penalty?

The situation usually results in offsetting fouls (fouls that cancel each other out) during the dead ball period between downs. This means that no yardage is walked off against either team. It is very difficult to single out individuals in a fight of this type. The important thing is to get the players settled down and then get the game going again.

Can each team use its own ball during the game?

In pro ball both teams use the balls supplied by the home team. This presents no problem because all pro teams are required by rule to use exactly the same style football, made by the same manufacturer. In college ball the teams may use a ball of their choice when they are in possession as long as the ball meets the specifications of the rule. The collegiate rules do not specify a particular ball, only that the ball meet the requirements described in the "ball" section of this book.

Is the amount of air that can be put into a football regulated by the rules, or is it up to the home team?

Both college and pro football require the ball to be filled with no less than 12½ pounds of air and not more than 13½ pounds of air. The weight of an official football is between 14 and 15 ounces.

Who checks the amount of air in the game balls?

In both college and pro ball the game footballs are presented to the officials at least one hour prior to the game. The officials check each ball with a pressure gauge, and if there is need for an air pump, it is supplied by the home management.

What would the game officials do if all the balls were used up in a high-scoring game?

This is a highly unlikely situation, but if all the balls were used up and it was not possible to get another one, the game would have to be suspended or canceled. If I were involved in such an incident, you can be sure that a ball would be found, even if it had to be obtained from a local store.

Do players wear special shoes when they are playing on artificial fields?

Actually, any legal football shoe can be worn on artificial fields. Some teams wear the conventional cleated shoes, with each shoe having seven hard rubber cleats. Other teams wear shoes specially developed for artificial surfaces. Each shoe has from ten to twenty short molded cleats and is very light in weight.

How does the college football draft work, and what is meant by trading a man for a draft choice?

The National Football League college player draft is held shortly after the season is over. The team with the poorest season record is given first choice in selecting the player they feel will do the most for their program. The other teams follow in order of their record. More than four hundred players are selected annually by the teams in the draft.

Trading a player for a draft choice is quite common and a bit of a gamble. One team gives a player and is paid with a draft choice.

Why did the pro league change its hashmarks, and how do they compare with college hashmarks?

Collegiate hashmarks are 17⅔ yards from the sideline, and any play that ends with the ball in a side zone (the area between sideline and hashmark) is next put in play at the hashmark. The pros have moved their hashmarks almost 23⅔ yards from the sideline or, to be exact, 70 feet 9 inches from the sideline. With only 18 feet 6 inches between pro hashmarks, offensive potential is greatly increased, with more room to run to either sideline. This is the reason for the change.

The pro field has a special mark on each 15-, 10-, and 5-yard line a few yards outside of the hashmarks. What are they used for?

This additional marking has been placed at each of the above yard lines exactly 10 feet 9 inches outside of the hashmarks. I wonder how many of you have noticed the mark. It is usually a dot or a slash. The purpose is to keep the punter away from the goal posts when the ball is snapped from the fifteen-yard line or closer to the goal line. Only on fourth-down plays will the ball be placed on the special marks instead of the hashmarks. The new hashmarks are 18 feet 6 inches apart, and the goal posts are the same 18 feet 6 inches apart. Without the new marker outside of the hashmarks, the kicker would be behind the goal post when he was kicking.

How wide is the neutral zone, and does it differ in pro and college ball?

The neutral zone is the space between the two lines of scrimmage and is determined by the length of the football when it is ready for play. The ball must be no shorter than 11 inches and no longer than 11¼ inches. The neutral zone is exactly the same in college and pro ball.

Is it true that Canadian pro football has twelve men on a team instead of eleven?

They do have twelve men on a team. The extra player is a back-field man, which gives Canadian ball an extra pass receiver. The extra receiver is necessary because there is no downfield blocking in Canadian ball, and a running game is almost impossible to develop.

Is the Canadian football field the same size as the American field?

The playing field in Canadian ball is 110 yards long and 65 yards wide. Our fields are 100 yards long and 53 yards 1 foot wide. Quite a difference.

How do all those dogs get on the football field?

A good question. I wish I knew, and I'm sure the stadium managements around the country would also like to know. No one has ever confessed to bringing a dog to a game, so I guess the question will go unanswered for another hundred years.

Is there a rating system for officials, and who does the rating?

In each crowd of fifty thousand to a hundred thousand fans, all eyes are usually on the players and the ball, with the exception of one solitary pair. These belong to the "observer," a most qualified individual who sits high in the press box watching every move the officials make. He grades them very carefully and files his ratings with the office governing the game he is observing. The "observer" is truly an integral part of any officiating program that is always striving for perfection.

Who is the head official in a football game, and is his salary greater than that of the other officials?

The referee is the head of each crew of officials, but all game officials have equal responsibilities during the game. The referee has the added job of enforcing the fouls and signaling to the press box and fans. He is paid no more than any other member of the crew because of his position.

The referee in college ball always wears a white hat, while the rest of the crew wear black hats. The pro officials all wear white hats. Why the difference?

No scientific reason. No complicated rule specifying that certain colors should be worn on the head. The difference is obviously dictated by the dress codes of the pro league and college conferences.

Do football officials always work the same position, or do they move around?

Most officials specialize. They usually work the same position in every game. When an official is beginning his career he usually works all positions until he finds the one that fits. From that point on he works at becoming an expert at his chosen position. All officials are of equal importance on the field.

Why does the referee give a preliminary signal?

A preliminary signal is a very important part of officiating mechanics. As soon as a foul is called the referee should give the preliminary signal to let the fans, coaches, and press box know what is going on. After the captain of the offended team has been consulted, the referee will enforce or decline the penalty and then give the final signal to both sides of the field.

Why does the referee give the signal for a foul to both sides of the field?

So the fans on both sides of the field get the information. It wouldn't be fair to give the signal to the press box side of the field only.

Do officials work in crews?

Some college conferences work their officials in crews, and others do not. The Big Ten uses the crew system, with the same officials working together each week. The pro league crews all the way through the season but splits them up during the playoffs.

Are football officials selected from certain areas of the country?

The pro officials are selected from all over the county. College officials are usually selected from the general area of the conference schools. The Big Ten selects officials from a seven-state area. The ten Conference schools are located in these seven states.

How do the families of officials feel about their men in striped shirts?

Mighty proud!

What is a pregame conference?

Officials work very hard to be mentally and physically ready for the football season. When it finally arrives, there is one final brush-up in preparation for the game. Either the night before the game or several hours prior to the kickoff, the game officials meet in conference to go over every possible situation that may pop up in the game. The pregame meeting puts a fine edge on the already "sharp" officials. The pregame conference is the mental warm-up before the action begins.

What happens if one or more game officials are injured during the game?

Major college football teams use five- or six-man crews to officiate their games. If an official is injured and unable to continue, the remaining officials augment their mechanics and finish the game. A few college conferences have an alternate official on the sideline, but most do not. In pro ball six officials are always used, and when an injury occurs the remaining men work the game. Alternates are not used during regular-season games, but they are used in all playoffs. This ensures a full six-man crew for playoffs, even if an official is injured.

Are there many injuries among the officiating ranks during a football season?

Football officials must be in excellent physical condition in order to keep up with today's game. Because of this fine state of health, both mental and physical, officials are rarely injured. They do come up with the usual sprains and pulled muscles, but it is very rare when an official is unable to complete a game.

What is an inadvertent or "quick" whistle?

An inadvertent or "quick" whistle is when an official blows his whistle before a play is over. It is an official's error and is completely covered in the rules of both college and pro ball.

A legal forward pass is in flight when an official inadvertently blows his whistle. What happens to the ball?

In pro ball, the ball is returned to the spot where the ball was snapped and the down is charged. If the pass were thrown on first down and a quick whistle were blown, it would be second down at the same line of scrimmage. In college ball, the ball is returned to the spot of the previous snap just as for the pros, except that the down is replayed.

A fumble or backward pass is loose on the ground when the official blows his whistle. Where is the ball put for the next play?

In pro ball, the ball is awarded to the fumbling or passing team at the spot of the ball at the time the whistle blew. In college ball, the ball is awarded to the fumbling or passing team at the spot where that team last had possession of the ball.

A runner is in the clear when an official blows his whistle. Where is the ball next put in play?

In both pro and college ball, the ball is dead where it is held by the runner when the whistle sounded.

A kick is in flight when the whistle blows. From what point will the ball next be snapped?

In pro ball, the receiving team would be awarded the ball at the spot of the ball at the time of the quick whistle. The officials will have to estimate the position of the ball when the whistle blew. In college ball, the ball will be returned to the spot of the previous snap and the down replayed.

Do officials have trouble hearing each other due to crowd noise?

When a crowd of seventy-five thousand fans are yelling at the tops of their voices, you can hardly hear yourself. Fortunately, officials have a language all their own. It is a wonderful set of arm signals that speak louder than the strongest bull horn. These signals are listed in this book, so learn them and get in on the conversation.

How do officials keep the ball dry in wet weather?

When the field is wet because of rain or snow, it is necessary to have a dry ball on each play. The ball boys or attendants send a dry ball into the game as soon as each down ends. The umpire then takes the ball and holds it or covers it until the teams are ready for play. The umpire does a great job of keeping the ball dry.

Do the officials like the artificial fields?

I can't speak for other officials, but I like the artificial fields. They are much easier to run on, and the surface is constant. You don't have to worry about stepping into a divot or slipping in the mud. In really bad weather an artificial field is a wonder to behold.

How do they put the lines on the artificial fields?

All of the lines on the artificial fields are painted. Unlike grass fields, which must be lined before each game, the artificial fields are usually painted twice during a football season.

Is it necessary to use a special down box and ten-yard chains on the artificial surfaces?

The conventional down box and chain poles are pointed on the end so they can be pushed into the ground. A special box and poles with suction cups or rubber tips are used on artificial fields because it would damage the surface if holes were punched in it.

Who trains new football officials?

There are hundreds of local officials' associations spread through-out the country. These associations usually meet once or twice a week from August through November, and they do a fine job of teaching new men how to officiate. The teachers are the veteran officials who must stay active in the local groups in order to per-petuate the profession.

When do officials begin getting ready for the next season?

I can't speak for other officials, but I begin preparation for the next season on the day after the current season ends. Officiating is a twelve-month avocation for me, and I am sure most other offi-cials would tell you the same thing.

How do officials get in shape for the season?

I can only speak for myself. I do a lot of running and bicycle rid-ing. I play tennis as often as I can, and most important, I push myself away from the dinner table before I eat too much. Condi-tioning at age twenty-five is like falling off a log, but when you are over thirty-five it's a lot of work. Each man has his own way of getting into shape. But he will be in shape for the season, and that is a promise.

Do officials work any football during the off-season?

Most officials work off-season scrimmages. On the college level there is more opportunity to work because of spring practice. Most major colleges have three- or four-game scrimmages and a final spring game during April and May. The pro officials don't have spring scrimmages, but they do work preseason scrimmages at the various training camps. Officials need practice just like the players do.

Do officials attend preseason meetings or clinics to brush up on new rules, etc.?

Officials actually study most of the year in preparation for the football season. They also attend a very complete clinic just prior to the start of the season. Officiating is definitely not just a 2½-hour job on Saturday, Sunday, or Monday night.

Can an official work pro and college football games in the same season?

College officials can work high school games as long as they do not work on the day prior to their college assignment, but are not allowed to work in the pro league. Pro officials cannot work anything but pro games.

Who assigns the officials for the college all-star football game?

The six officials who work the College All-Star football game are assigned by the National Football League. The game is played under pro rules, and it should be officiated by pro officials.

Who selects the game officials for college bowl games?

The officials are assigned by the college conferences that are represented in the bowl games. If a bowl participant is an independent, they usually have their officials assigned by a major college conference.

How do you feel just before a football game begins?

Last fall I wrote a few lines on the subject, so I'll just repeat them for you now:
  "Last Saturday afternoon at ten minutes past one I walked from the long tunnel into the University of Michigan Memorial

Stadium. The weather was perfect for a football game, and I could feel the electricity of this enormous crowd of 104,000 fans. It was just minutes from the start of the traditional Michigan-Michigan State rivalry game, always one of the highlights of the Big Ten football season. The ever-present 'butterflies' were at work in my stomach, and my own excitement grew as kickoff time drew near. This feeling of wonderful anxiety just before each game is indescribable. Other football officials know the feeling, and if you have ever competed, you know it too. I wouldn't trade these pregame moments for anything in the world."

INDEX

CREDITS

ILLUSTRATIONS: Jack Jordan, Jack Ryan

JACKET PHOTOGRAPHS: Edgar A. Feldman, M.D.

FULL-PAGE CARTOONS: Cramer Products, Gardner, Kansas

BIBLIOGRAPHY

Bonham, Howard B., *Football Lingo,* Memphis: Diversified Publishing Co., 1962.

National Collegiate Athletic Association, *Official Football Rules, 1972, 1973.* Phoenix.

Official Rules for Professional Football, 1972 NFL 1973 Rules Changes. New York.

Otto, J. R., *Football,* Mankato, Minnesota: Creative Educational Society, Inc., 1961.

Rydell, Wendell, *Football,* New York: Abelard-Schuman Ltd., 1971.